WHITE / BLACK
MAN / MAN

WHITE MAN / BLACK MAN

Michael Keating
and
Jimmy Watson

PRAEGER PUBLISHERS
New York · Washington

Published in the United States of America in 1974
by Praeger Publishers, Inc.
111 Fourth Avenue, New York, N.Y. 10003

Library of Congress Cataloging in Publication Data

Keating, Michael.
  White man, Black man.

    1. Keating, Michael. 2. Watson, Jimmy. 3. Journalists—Correspon-
dence, reminiscences, etc. I. Watson, Jimmy. II. Title.
PN4874.K37A38   070'.92'2   73-1093
ISBN 0-275-19760-7

Printed in the United States of America

To Kate

Acknowledgments

These people, in particular, contributed to the creation of this book. They provided either inspiration, assistance in the production, or financial help in times of stress: Dr. Leonard Kriegel, Susan Needles, William P. Keating, Mary Robinson, Arline Borders, Sharon Ferguson, Jean Rinklin, Kara Keating, Martha Keating, David Butwin, June Rook. Léon King, editor of this book, contributed greatly and creatively to its form. Thank you all, friends.

Introduction

It's a wrench for a journalist to arrive at a point where he decides that the most interesting story he knows is his own. All of his professional experience has been in telling the stories of others, keeping himself concealed beneath his byline and his journalistic standards.

Then when Jimmy Watson found me after a separation of a few years and told me he had a story to tell—well! It dawned on me.

Both of our stories were unusual yet in many ways typical of our times; unconventional yet illustrative of convention, similar to the dilemma of many achievement-oriented men today; why not tell those stories together, make them one?

That idea answered certain problems. With someone else involved in the writing of my autobiography my terror of self-exposure was diminished; and writing with me lightened Jimmy's terror at the whole prospect of writing anything. He had never written for publication.

So in the beginning of winter, 1972, Jimmy and I decided we would do that—we would write our own stories in conjunction with each other and in the same book, and I would teach Jimmy to write as the project went along. We had only the vaguest idea how the story would develop, how the two lives would mesh, how we would work with each other.

"We'll let it grow like a tree," Jimmy suggested on that first day of our decision.

MICHAEL KEATING

New York
February, 1974

Notice

Some of the people and some of the events described in this book have been modified to protect the identities, and in some cases the lives, of individuals. Dialogue is reconstructed from memory.

THE AUTHORS

WHITE / BLACK
MAN / MAN

1 "What should I wear? I can wear pants can't I?"
"Honey, you can wear anything you want so long as you look *good*. This guy I'm gonna meet is a friend, so don't overdo it like you're dressing up for a big occasion."

LaVaughn was five feet, two inches of dynamite. She had come to Great Neck from Mobile, Alabama, six years ago.

"Can Wendy come?"

"Sure, Baby. Call her."

Wendy was LaVaughn's closest friend.

I had called Mike a few hours earlier and arranged to meet him at his apartment. I had only seen Mike twice in the years following my brief tenure at CBS. This was to be our second meeting within ten days. At our last meeting I had barely recognized him.

His soft, boyish face seemed transformed, as though a sculptor, with only his thumbs and chisel, had redone his work.

The eyes, while retaining their radiant blue, were gouged deeper, reflecting more pain, more sorrow. The cheeks, once round, were now sunken a little, lean, and lined with time and experience.

3

His whole physical appearance had been through a process of evolution. Gone were those impeccably correct business suits, shirts, ties, mannerisms, and speech. John Glenn had suddenly gone haywire, smashed his instrument panel, ripped off his space suit, put on a loin cloth, belted Pat Nixon over the head with a club, grabbed a fistful of her hair, and dragged her off to Pike's Peak. I had always sensed the presence of another being cradled inside him, an infant being that became visible whenever he had had a few scotches and smiled.

We stepped out of our apartment and felt the cool dampness of the wintry Long Island Sound blowing in underneath the garage door.

Me and LaVaughn were shacking in a one-bedroom basement apartment at 51 Sham Avenue. Underworld underground. It felt funny living among so many white people, probably because I was a heroin supplier and white folks is nosy, especially about new cars, new niggers, and their neighborhood. I stayed in during white folks' working hours and came out late at night when they would be fucking or sleeping.

As my big Olds cruised toward where Wendy would be waiting for us, I gave LaVaughn more background on Mike.

"Baby, I'm telling you this guy I can't believe. If you'd known him three years ago and saw him now; he's beautiful."

"Oh, yeah? Why?"

"Long story. Used to be a big-time dude at CBS. I used to work for him."

"Stop. There she is."

We picked up Wendy and started for the city.

We crossed the Triboro Bridge into Manhattan, then turned downtown at Seventh Avenue and 125th Street. There was a stop I wanted to make before we got to Mike's. I had to see No-Ko.

We exited Central Park at 72d Street. At 74th and Broadway I found a space and parked. He was across the street

4

shivering—he had been waiting in the cold—I was twenty minutes late. He waited for me to cross then turned and started up the block. About midway up the street he stopped and placed his hand on a can overflowing with garbage, then came back to me. He was high as a motherfucker. He barely whispered "Dyno, my man" as he reached for the extended twenty-dollar bill and continued on his way.

It was in the garbage can, right on top, four bags of Colombian reefer. No-Ko never beat you. He was an honest businessman—a rarity in the streets. No-Ko was twelve.

A few minutes later we were parking in front of Mike's house. As we entered the building, one of those wide, high structures on Riverside Drive overlooking the Hudson River, the doorman eyed me like I was some kind of pimp, bringing two fine black bitches up to "Mr. Keating's apartment." He looked like he didn't like it, but his look would change if I was coming to his pad.

Mike answered the buzzer with a triumphant flourish, like he was fucked up and we were welcome to get fucked up with him. But we were already fucked up, sniffing and smoking in the car. Stepping into the living room was an experience; acid rock, one of his new freedoms, was pumping out from a boss stereo set. Daring posters, alive with color, excited my imagination and electrified my body.

I felt my pants bulge warm and stiff for a moment when I looked—not glanced, looked—at two lovely women, bare to the upper waist, one with her lips sweetly drawing and giving sensation to the other's breast. There were posters of love and freedom, but that one I remembered best.

"Man, I got some out of sight grass. Have some of this."

I took the joint Mike had been smoking. I was high already but I had been smoking long enough to know good pot when I tasted it, and this was class-A garbage. I hated to do it but when he asked me how it was, smiling and somehow sure that my reply would support his claim, I told him it wasn't shit.

That was unexpected.

5

"Jimmy always has to have the best drugs," he responded. "Nobody's going to have better drugs than him."

I sensed that he might have taken my reply as a put-down, because it was obvious that he was making his speech more for the girls than for me—I was commenting on the smoke, he was commenting on me.

But if the girls had chosen to judge his statement, they would have held that his words were true. It was true to the extent that I always wanted to know who had or could get the best, so I could have the best.

I offered him some of No-Ko's grass, and once Mike took hold of that joint it worked its magic on him. He got high. This seemed to make him think he was the only person in the room that was high.

"Come on. Give some dope to the girls."

I convinced him they were stoned already. He dug that. "That's good man. What's next?"

It was as good a time to begin as any. He was glowing with anticipation. I dropped down and stretched out on the rug, drawing LaVaughn down with me.

"Eh, my man," I said, looking up at him, "I got an idea. Why don't we write a book together?"

*　*　*

I was back there a few months ago on an assignment for a magazine—a travel story on the City of Montreal, my birth-place and home for the first twenty years of my life.

Two decades later, and the place had hardly changed. There was a new front door on the large house on Strath-cona Avenue in which I grew up—a modern door with two slits of glass in the wood—and a strange family was inside. The house had been sold by my father long ago, when most of his seven children had moved away and he had fallen on hard times after World War II ended and Canada no longer needed a navy or the marine hardware my father had manu-

6

factured in a steaming, banging factory in Pointe St. Charles
with a smokestack of red bricks encasing yellow bricks
that spelled out for a mile around: K E A T I N G.

No, nothing much had changed on Strathcona Avenue.
Nor had much changed in the city of Westmount, the English-
speaking enclave surrounded by French-speaking Montreal.
Westmount would never change, of course. Westmounters
would sit in their stone houses on the side of the hill until
the Frenchmen blew them up, as they recently tried to do.
There was, though, in Westmount now a fancy plaza erected
over the Westmount stop of Montreal's crisp and swift new
subway.

St. Leo's Academy was in the same place—a walk away
from Strathcona Avenue. It was in a new building now.
Thank God for that. Did the school still have the white
line in the hallway separating the English side of the school
from the French side? The French-speaking boys went to
St. Leo's Church at the bottom of the block, the English-
speaking to Ascension Church at the head of the block—the
perfect Westmount order, where the English spoke English
to everyone, including the Frenchmen. "Pepsis," we called
them.

The trees on Strathcona Avenue were still there, lining
each side of the street, providing a summertime shade can-
opy that cooled the lawns and the pavement so that the
blistering heat of Montreal summers passed by unnoticed
during those few weeks out of school waiting to go to camp
or the cottage in the Laurentien Mountains. In the fall the
trees blanketed the street with russet leaves that we'd heap
into huge piles along the curb. We'd haul our wagons up
the slope of the street and, face down upon them, careen
down into the leaves, suffocating in the rich smell of softly
decaying foliage until my mother called me as the first
touches of evening darkened the street.

During the war there were blackouts in Westmount for
simulated air raids. My oldest brother was a gunner in the

7

RCAF, and my sisters brought English pilots home for dinner.

My father loved to argue. He would argue with the English pilots at the dinner table. I would listen with confusion, adoring the pilots, dreaming of them bailing out of flaming planes, and growing silently angry at my father's anti-Semitism and Irish hostility toward all things English.

"Your great grandfather was dragged from his sickbed by the English and shot against a wall. Never forget that," my father would say.

"Hush, Will," my mother would say in the midst of one of his harangues of the English pilots, "or they'll put you on St. Helen's Island."

The mayor of Montreal was interned on St. Helen's Island for the duration. He had been urging young French Canadian men to resist the draft. I had the nagging fear that my father would go to internment camp. He didn't, though. He bought himself a 60-foot schooner—it was built in his smokestack factory—said to be the largest yacht in Montreal at the time. It drew 7½ feet, so we often ran aground on shallow Lake St. Louis. Senior members of the Royal St. Lawrence Yacht Club referred to my father as Hard Aground Keating. He didn't care about running aground, because by the time we'd cast off from the mooring a fifth of Johnny Walker was warming his humor (he said he had been in his cabin looking at the charts for the day), and there were lots of children and in-laws to winch the boat off the rocks, and the boat's heavy lead keel couldn't be damaged.

Great boisterous Sunday dinners on Strathcona Avenue with children, in-laws, lovers, friends, a mountainous rump roast sliced transparent thin by my father, boiled carrots chopped into small pieces and soaked in butter and salt, and mounds of whipped potatoes in which I hid little pats of butter, then hunted for buried treasure with a fork, finding small pools of gold which dripped onto my pants' leg as forkful after forkful headed toward my mouth, where they lay limp on my tongue, melting finally into a shiver of contentment.

A lusty family where the boys peeked in the keyhole of the bathroom door while sisters were showering and I was strapped at age six for putting sticks up the vagina of the little girl from the house on the other side of Strathcona Avenue while she looked on fascinated, neither of us noticing my father's angry face peering in the basement window at us.

Always lots of liquor and flirtation among the sisters and brothers and a front porch overloaded with young men jostling each other for the attention of my glamorous sisters. And a constant chatter about sex, sex, sex; with amusement among the children but with a hard lascivious edge outside the group where the priests kept flagellating our libidos. The priests. God! They were incessant on the subject—at school, from the pulpit, in the confessional as I counted aloud in their hairy ears the number of times I had masturbated. (I didn't, however, tell them all the glorious details of the starlit night six of the boys on Strathcona Avenue stretched out on one of our front lawns under a three-quarter moon and en masse jerked each other off. Or of the sixty girls locked up in my fantasy harem, each one abject in the face of my demanding desires and the whip I flicked in my right hand.)

No one noticed me very much—the sixth of seven children can be obscure merely by keeping quiet—and I slipped through St. Leo's Academy without a ruffle, excelling in spelling and reading, and reading every book in the house on Strathcona Avenue, including all of Sinclair Lewis. Lewis taught me a new way of looking at adults and their activities. Most of them seemed to be Babbitts, and I resolved never to become one myself.

After elementary school and puberty, ennui overcame me and I regularly began to fail in school, transferring from one to another, only half-conscious of the variety of classrooms I was put into by my exasperated father.

9

"He should learn a trade," I would hear my father say to my mother. But my mother insisted on another school, another try, and she prevailed.

My parents, brothers, and sisters began calling me "unconscious," and my father demanded I join the St. Leo's boxing team, where my lips would get cut even though we used heavily padded gloves. Then on Saturday mornings he would wait until I rigged myself in a red, white, and green St. Leo's bantam football uniform. Then he would drive me in full regalia to Westmount Park and wait until I joined the squad in practice on the large green field. There was no escape then, so I would play. If he had other things to do and couldn't wait, I would slip off into the trees, sit around for a few hours, muddy my face, and go home. I had the sense that I wasn't turning out the way my father wanted, and we hardly ever talked about me.

He did talk often about his boyhood in Newfoundland and his love of the sea and the seafaring life.

"It's a clean life," he said. "There's nothing like salt air, salt water. The sea. It's a clean life."

So at sixteen I left school and shipped out on the RMS *Lady Nelson* as a utility boy, washing dishes in a steam-filled cubbyhole off the first-class dining room. Fine times sailing to the Caribbean and Guiana! Mount Gay rum and Coca Cola in waterfront bars, and pimps plucking at my sleeve. It finally happened in a rattan bar in Guiana when a whore about my age sat on my lap, took my hand, and placed it on her right tit. We were upstairs within minutes, her crimson dress on the floor, and her chocolate body waiting on the stained bed. It took, oh, maybe thirty seconds and the veil was rent, the mystery pierced. I was a man. Oh boy!

It was a whorehouse in every port after that, rum and music. Growth.

The passage from the ship to the street in Georgetown, British Guiana, was through a long warehouse made sweetly nauseating by the smell of molasses. I was alone, heading for a night in the bars. The warehouse fronted on a small square surrounded on three sides by other blank-walled warehouses, and on the fourth side a narrow passageway between buildings led to the street. The usual crowd of vendors had their crates set up in the small square selling bay rum, raw rubber figurines, monkeys, and sometimes their sisters, or so they said. I'd been through there a half-dozen times since the ship made port two days before, so I didn't stop at the vendors this time.

"Hold it, mon." It was said softly from behind my back. I turned around and met the gaze of a boy, black and a couple of years older than myself. He held a knife waist high, the point aimed at me.

"You gave me a lotta shit this afternoon, mon. You're gonna get yours now."

He had been stopping sailors inside the warehouse that afternoon, asking for money, saying he was a sailor on the beach. My companion had never been to Georgetown before, so I was showing him the ropes, showing him how to handle the beggars.

"If you're a sailor on the beach, you gotta have a union card," I had told the beggar. "Where's your card?"

He didn't have one, and I told him to get lost.

"Pretty big this afternoon with all that shit about union cards, mon. You don't look so big now. I'm gonna get you, mon."

He stood in front of me, unmoving. The knife still pointed at my stomach. I didn't move and stared back at him, saying nothing. Inside I had gone blank and cold; scared.

The vendors lifted their heads from their wares and watched. No one else was in the square. Me, the boy, and the vendors. Everybody was black but me.

I waited for him to move. "I'm gonna get you, mon," he said again, but he didn't move.

11

Time passed.

A few of the vendors drifted over; two of them spoke softly from behind my back: "We're with you, mon. We're with you." A couple more came over. "We're with you, mon." They spoke just above a whisper.

The boy looked at me again, then turned on his heel, put away his knife, and walked down the narrow lane to the street. I waited a moment, looked at the vendors, and silently made my way to the street.

I hadn't flinched. The rum and the girls tasted good that night.

But there was a constant negative amid the carousing and the sweeping sea sunrises—the continually refreshed memory of that night before the first voyage began; the night in Montreal when the ship's headwaiter, after an evening of buying drinks, placed his soft hand on my leg while we sat on the steps of a Montreal church stabilizing the alcohol spinning in my head. There was no protest from me when his manicured fingers crept up my thigh and slipped into my fly. He led me the three blocks to the ship and his cabin. I left in the morning and took an hour-long shower.

Word of the headwaiter's conquest spread throughout the ship after we were at sea, and soon everyone it seemed was picking at the fly of the fresh boy aboard. It became in the end pursuit and flight—a horror. So, after three months at sea and two voyages to South America, I returned to St. Leo's Academy to finish high school. This time I went out for the football team without my father's prodding. I felt estranged and bored, pressed in and intimidated by the strength and numbers of my brothers and sisters, and I was crude with the girls I met.

After high school, I tried a year of a Jesuit college in Montreal, flunked out, then left the city for a college in Nova Scotia. My mother had managed to get me in despite my father's demand again that I learn a trade. My mother at that time was in the midst of a series of cerebral strokes that would close down her mind long before her eventual death.

Except for visits and funerals, I never went home again.

❖ ❖ ❖

I wrote poetry, short stories, newspaper features, became the leading man on stage, formed a radical political party, drank, gave parties, rarely studied, and dressed eccentrically at St. Francis Xavier University in Antigonish, Nova Scotia, a small town by the sea dominated by the Catholic cathedral of the bishop who resided there.

The sons of miners, fishermen, the petit bourgeois from Canada's maritime provinces and a few New England states attended St. Francis Xavier, where the college taught them that they should be masters of their own destiny. It was a working-class college fired with a sense of practical mission: to teach the students and their parents the way to achieve control over their own lives despite capitalism. Its sense was contained in the practice of the Antigonish Movement —higher education was not to be used as a device for escaping one's social class. In other words, the college hoped that a miner's son would not, after getting his degree, move on to law school or medical school and establish a wealthy practice in Halifax, never to return to Cape Breton. Instead, the college hoped he would return to his village and become a local leader, organizing the disfranchised and teaching them to beat the system. The device used was the cooperative movement, and the college faculty went about the countryside teaching rudimentary economics and labor theory to the fishermen, farmers, and laborers, teaching them to organize their own sales of their labor, to free themselves of their indenture to the owners of wealth. Along with their sons, the fathers came to the campus, too, for thirty-day "short courses" on organizing cooperatives. Governments of

13

impoverished provinces in India and South America sent students to learn the techniques.

The working-class atmosphere was exotic to a dandy from Montreal. While I took little part in movement activities, I watched and learned.

Toward the end of my junior year at St. Francis Xavier I met a young girl from the women's college atop a nearby hill. She was from upstate New York, blonde, beautiful, sensual, and first in her class. We went out a lot together that spring, and when the school year ended we necked on the crowded train all the way to New Brunswick. We had to change trains there, she to go south to New York State, I to continue west to Victoria, British Columbia, to train as an officer cadet with the Royal Canadian Navy.

We said goodby on the platform. Tears wetted my cheeks as her train left. It was the first time I had cried with love, and I sensed another beginning. I was awed and thrilled by it. At the end of the summer I drove back across the continent to her home in Vernon, New York, and asked her to marry me. She did, a month after my graduation, and I moved to the United States where there seemed to be more action. Canada looked dull by comparison.

✿　✿　✿

It had been fast movement upward, excitement and change. Four children and Editorial Director of WCBS-TV, the Columbia Broadcasting System's "flagship" station, the one William S. Paley and Frank Stanton watched, the country's Number One television station.

Oh, there had been a pause or two since I left Montreal. There had been the time when I had just turned thirty and had decided that I was rotting in a going-nowhere job with the Associated Press in Albany. Those day trips on the bus to New York every month, knocking on the doors of CBS, NBC, *New York Times, New York Herald*

14

Tribune. Nothing had happened for over a year, and I went every month. That had been a pause, a depression.

But only a pause. Eventually the *Herald Tribune* offered, I accepted, and it was off around the country covering the 1964 presidential election, front page on the *Trib* every day, and after a year an offer from CBS—$6,000 more per annum. I needed the money; the kids were enlarging.

And now, Sunday night after skiing, everyone glowing. My wife in the process of putting together her own public relations and advertising agency in Midtown—money in the bank, a few stocks, a boat at the World's Fair Marina under canvas for the winter, and, yes, my presence on those thousands of TV sets every night, saying intelligent things about the state of the city, the state, the country, the world.

The sanitation trucks would not wake us up early tomorrow. I had mentioned to my friend the Sanitation Commissioner that the trucks at 7:15 below our windows woke us up too early. Now the trucks arrived on 105th Street after 8 o'clock.

And Monday, Tuesday, Wednesday, Thursday, and Friday mornings the subway about 10, after the rush hour, to Midtown and a quick, bright walk to Avenue of the Americas, an office on the twenty-fifth floor with a view of the Jersey side of the Hudson, writing, meeting, talking about the state of the world, then a late afternoon walk across 57th Street to Broadcast Center to tape the evening's comments, and afterward a martini with a girl friend. Maybe dinner for two, or ten.

And always the public issues—school strikes, state budgets, gubernatorial elections, police brutality, drug abuse, government reorganization, invasion of privacy, the flight to the suburbs, governmental efficiency, tax dollars, economic policy, health care, war on poverty, Vietnam, the Middle East, assassinations, right wing, left wing, liberal, conservative . . . sensible solutions poured forth from me nightly.

Then Harlem burned, Newark burned, Detroit burned,

Chicago, Los Angeles. As the Editorial Director of WCBS-TV I was confronted with the necessity of formulating the station's position on this phenomenon, which cut through acres of sloughy clichés and forced whites in the North to deal more truly with their real attitudes toward blacks.

Within the television industry, immensely prosperous at the time, there were two basic reactions, similar to the reactions of white America in general.

ONE: The niggers have been agitated by the bleeding hearts of the liberal left, which gives them handouts instead of sweat-of-the-brow work, and the niggers should be shot if they take as much as a transistor radio they didn't pay for.

TWO: Negroes locked in the ghettos are venting their justified frustrations on a system that has failed to provide them with a decent standard of living and integration with us nice folk, and with a little jiggling of the system here and a little more cash and some jobs there, all will be well again, and we can all get back to business.

The latter position was the only one discussed by the WCBS-TV Editorial Board. If some of the members of the board felt otherwise they didn't let on.

The board met every week for an hour or two in a windowless meeting room tucked away in a corner near the elevators on the twenty-fifth floor of Black Rock, the black granite CBS corporate headquarters on the Avenue of the Americas at 52d Street. The meetings usually carried through noon, so we'd send out to the Brasserie for a box lunch, French style, and discuss THE ISSUES over cheese and apples.

The General Manager of the station presided over the Editorial Board. He would be one of a passing parade of ambitious, bright, button-down, well-spoken television time salesmen from out of town, around forty, give or take a few years on either side of that difficult age, brought into New York not to run a station—Paley and Stanton did that—but to show themselves to the men who would decide whether

16

they then would step up to the next rung, the one that meant, with deft management of stock options, millionaire-dom. Some made it, some didn't, and during the wait these decision-makers infected the station and its personnel with their knuckle-cracking, lip-biting, left-knee-jiggling tension and fear.

So it became the lot of the Editorial Director to distract the General Manager from time to time from his pressing concerns to seek approval for the station's public stance on a public issue. Since the General Manager had usually arrived in town only a short while before, my function at the Editorial Board meetings often became not so much the initiator of a reasoned argument over a controversy as a monologist telling the boss what was going on in his new town. The other members of the board, men whose responsibilities were in other areas of the station—news, programing, public relations—did the same, everyone tumbling over themselves to display to the latest boss how much they knew of the inner workings of New York City, establishing their public issue credentials. With each new boss I would sit back and listen to my associates trundle out their worn stories about what the Mayor said on this private occasion, and what their good friend Commissioner So and So had to say off the record about this and that.

Most times the board meetings seemed foolish. After all, editorializing on the air was what I had been hired to do, and because of my professional background as a political and government reporter I was obviously the most qualified to do it. But the board meetings had to be held, because the company insisted that the General Manager be responsible for the editorial policies of his station even though everyone knew better. So we all played the solemn game, once a week.

The ghetto riots, however, confronted the members of the Editorial Board with an issue that involved them on many levels, from disruption of their own programing with special reports on the crisis to concern about their own and their families' security. So the Editorial Board discussions, for a change, were laden with concern, concern that became more pressing when in March 1968 the National Commission on Civil Disorders reported that the country was becoming more and more two separate societies, one white and one black. We weren't coming together at all!

And, oh, most difficult of all, exposure of the dirty little secret of the mass media—that less than 5 per cent of the people in the news profession were black, and that white journalists had no interest in nor connection with black events or persons.

The press, the report said, "repeatedly, if unconsciously, reflects the biases, the paternalism, the indifference of white America. This may be understandable, but it is not excusable in an institution that has the mission to inform and educate the whole of our society."

So there it was, splashed all over the front pages and on the network news, and the readers and viewers who had been turning against the hypocrisy of the media had more evidence now with which to condemn the bearers of bad tidings. And there was no sloughing off the criticism, because it came from one of those establishment, blue-ribbon commissions that editorial writers always clamored for in times of national stress. Furthermore, the racism was obvious to everyone, inside and outside the profession.

The schedule of Editorial Board meetings was accelerated, and we discussed what we called the minority hiring problem. At first the familiar refrain was expressed—handwringing about the lack of qualified blacks and everyone reassuring each other of his good intentions. That was not enough, because it was dawning on the hierarchy of CBS that hiring practices had better change lest the issue turn into challenges to those precious television station licenses that CBS owned and that produced such enormous revenue for the corporation.

So from the top on down it was impressed upon the various divisions of CBS, especially the broadcast divisions, that more minorities needed to be employed and that the various managers would be held responsible for making this happen.

There was the feeling at that time that changing the complexion of the company required only an expression of good intentions, that all CBS needed to do was to state that black is beautiful and suddenly—shazam—black people would be functioning at all levels of the company. They forgot about the many people involved in the hiring and promotion practices of a large company. And they were unaware of the deep suspicion that blacks had of white institutions and promises of employment.

To personnel interviewers, the people-processors, blacks were at best exotic and odd and at worst dangerous ne'er-do-wells who would lift your wallet or pocketbook the moment you turned your chair around to get an application blank out of the drawer of the cabinet behind your desk.

And the way those people dressed. My gawd, Bill! Lavender shirts, no ties, cocks and balls bulging through crotches of too tight iridescent red pants, and forests of kinky hair which make them look like, yes I remember now, those man-eaters from the jungle comic books. Sheena, Queen of the Jungle, was the lithe female, tiger skin just skimming and concealing the place of adolescent fixation where her long and lovely thighs joined and you knew that if you could just lift the tiger skin you would find gloriously shimmering pubic hair like that which started at the top of her blonde head and ended at the small of her arched back, not an end of it split. Yes, jungle queens were always blonde, we remember, and the lurking rapists peering through the overhanging branches by the river where she was bathing, nipples just below the surface of the water and her tiger skin hanging on a tree, well, you know what color they were.

And the way they spoke at interviews. Who would understand the accent, the mumbling and drawling? And to the routine question on the application—have you ever been convicted of a crime?—many yeses to that.

The attitude, too. The attitude maybe worst of all. These

19

people didn't come on smiling and selling, putting their best feet forward and gleaming with grooming. No, they either hung back in nervous alienation and suspicion, or they came on with the weaving and the shoulder-dipping, hip-clicking, supercilious street bopster cool, trying to conceal their certainty that there wouldn't be any jobs here for black folk except maybe sifting the white sand in the ashtrays by the elevator doors on each of the floors in the CBS building. And Dr. Stanton wanted us to hire these people to walk the upholstered black walls and italianate white vinyl floors of Black Rock, where even the pictures hanging on the walls of an administrator, executive salary grade 1, had to be approved by an art committee staffed probably by the mistresses of vice presidents? What was the world coming to, anyway?

A General Manager swiveled his chair in his corner office with floor-to-ceiling windows gazing in two directions over the roofs of Midtown Manhattan in the middle of a closed-circuit broadcast from one of James Brown's first television appearances, nodded in the direction of the set, and said to me: "Look at that animal."

So the process of changing the complexion of CBS went along turgidly there at the start, and some of the blacks who came into the company were not happy with suggestions to cut their Afros.

Blacks were not clamoring to get into CBS, and nothing was happening. Frank Stanton decided then, or was pushed into deciding, to actually hire blacks, not merely say that he wanted to hire blacks. So to the heads of all divisions a memorandum was sent bearing Frank Stanton's initials, that elegantly interlocked FS that scared the shit out of everyone, stating that the personnel roster of the company must reflect the ethnic makeup of the communities in which the units of the company operated. Each division president was ordered to provide Stanton each quarter with a report on the racial makeup of the employees in each division un-

20

der his charge. He expected, he said, that each report would show growth in the percentage of minority employees.

It had to be on paper now, with graphs showing growth. Memos explaining the unavailability of applicants no longer were acceptable. So within a few months, after all those years of complaints about the lack of qualified candidates and where do you find them and they can't read or write, black people, mostly black women, appeared in Black Rock. Almost overnight, it seemed, the rows of secretaries on the twenty-fifth floor where I worked took on a chocolate hue. Surprise! Surprise! It turned out not to be that difficult after all. It took only a memo from Frank Stanton telling his subordinates get some blacks or it's your ass, and the blacks moved up from the mailroom.

In this atmosphere, I was successful in selling to the General Manager and the president of the Television Stations Division an idea that had been formulating in my mind—an apprenticeship program under which the station would seek out young black people, either in high school or in college, interest them in becoming journalists, train them, and give them a job.

The general outline of the idea was accepted without difficulty. I was commissioned to design the program and run it, in addition to my editorial work. It was to be for me a journey to another land, and I never saw my own again in the same way.

Jimmy Watson was among those I recruited.

✿　✿　✿

When I first knew that CBS was going to interview me for a job I knew that I would get it. Things had been going my way and I felt lucky. But I didn't know whether I wanted it or not.

Working for CBS would make Momma happy, my wife and kids happy, Momma-in-Law, Pop-in-Law, Step-Pop, Pop.

Shit, everybody would be happy! Me? I didn't know. I'd been doing things that other people wanted me to do for so long that I didn't know now what made me happy except smoking, sniffing, and fucking, in that order and all together. When I was in the Marine Corps I did what I wanted most of the time and survived because I knew what they wanted. The service teaches you not to know what you want. It teaches you to perceive what others want of you. And a few other lessons—like talking tough to some white boys in Georgia when I was on leave. The speckle-faced cracker had a pistol in his hand when he pulled over to the side of the highway and yelled: "Git in here, nigger!" There wasn't no trial. The white boy said I was the one who had cussed him and the speckle-faced cracker delivered me to a work farm. I cried that night in the shit-filled air of the pen—why was these white folks doing this to me? Ol' Amos made the other six dudes in the pen stop teasing me. "Dey cain't keep yuh mo' den thutty days, boy, so hesh up now and take it lak a MAN!" I stopped crying then, but five days later the food gave me diarrhea. That night, chained in my corn-shuck bunk, lying in my own shit, I cried again. And hated!

I knew the CBS job would mean close contacts with whites on their terms—terms I was sure I wouldn't like. I thought about my mother who wanted so much for me. If I wanted the CBS job to make someone happy it would have to be her. She wanted so much for me. She had sent me for singing piano lessons at Mrs. Pearson's with the few dollars she earned doing day work. Good old Mrs. Pearson. She had my mother convinced that I had talent: "That son of yours gonna be a star one day, Mrs. Watson." My mother kept them two dollars flowing.

I did make it in a play at the Roxy Theater for two days. My part called for me to run across the stage, grab some big fat bitch 'round the knees, and on my knees yell out: "Mammy! Mammy! Don't let them take me!"

Years later I realized I had played the part of a slave. But back then I was in the spotlight. Everybody told me how good I was—I loved it! It was true, I could be anything I wanted. My mother said so—until I took the test for the Bronx High School of Science.

I passed but was told that many others had passed with higher scores and the quota was filled. My mother came to school bitching, so some school big shit told her that I was eligible for Stuyvesant but they only had room for one more and their pick was Ivan Greiletzer because of his "superior conduct." My mother told him that was "bullshit. . . . Greiletzer was a Jew!" What the fuck was his superior conduct? I knew damn well I was just as smart or smarter. Ain't nobody gonna tell me that shit when I knew all I had ever seen in either one of those schools was white boys, a lot of them with those little black skull caps on their heads, and a couple of hi yaller boys with curly hair, nothing as dark as me.

Well, I had made up for that when I got into City College, kept up with them smart Jew kids, and got real high grades. Shit, I was almost Super Nigger now.

Now here was CBS saying: Hey, nigger, you want a prestige job? Almost as good as Hollywood. Air-conditioned, fine ho's, glamour, op-po-tune-nitee. You damn right I want that job. It was paying off at last—all those prayers my mother said she said for me.

I laughed into the phone when "Poopie," my wife Ava, answered.

"I got the first interviews with the white folks made, baby."

"I knew it," she cooed back. "You always do it, baby." My Mama sure knew how to keep a man trying. She was thin, on the better side of skinny, big doe-like eyes, thin white-girl lips, big nose, long straight black hair, peanut tits, cute ass, straight legs, a fine motherfucker. Best of all she was a Libra like me. Yeah, that sweetass Ava. We'd been married ten years now but it seemed longer. She'd been my woman since she was ten and I was twelve. I'd seen her mailing a letter, walked over, told her my name, and said: "I'm gonna marry you!" And she knew I meant it.

Ava was a bona fide hi yaller. Both her mother and father were hi yallers. She was a spoiled bitch as most hi yallers were at that time. They held the best jobs and were always around someone with money. When the white folks asked them, "You're not Nee-grow are you?" they became everything but. Indians mostly, but also South Americans, Jamaicans, anything would do except Negro! Didn't nobody want to be that if they could help it. I copped out myself to being only half a nigger. I was too dark to be no-nigger, so half a nigger was better than whole nigger.

I went through all the antics and pretenses of being just what Whitey wanted. I charmed, delighted, was witty and *grinned*, but I wasn't humble Willie Mays style. Their dumbass questions and faces were forgotten as soon as their office doors closed. Only one counted anyway now. Keating. 6:55 P.M. Channel Two Editorial. I knew him. I saw him on TV.

I was really up—alert and quick—when the interview with Mike came off. I walked into his office and felt like I was walking into an icehouse. He looked and acted just like he did on TV—cool, matter-of-fact, and no bullshit. Like some fresh-ass captain from the Inspector General's office or something.

He asked me some shit about wher're you from? What your folks do for a living? Where're they from originally? What the fuck did he care? Did he really give a shit? I shot him some shit about sharecropping parents—playing on Whitey's sympathy. I'd been interviewed so many times by white folks that I could answer by reflex, mind calculating instantly what and how to answer, what pitch, what facial expression, what pause, etc. It was a game niggers and Whitey engaged in to the single satisfaction of Whitey.

Who the fuck wants to answer a lot of stupid questions by some paleface motherfucker you never seen before and don't see unless you're in trouble.

24

2 Across the yard from where I was sitting, staring out over the low black railing that surrounded my back porch, the rear of a sagging line of dirty red brick tenements leaned against one another like a row of musty old books about to fall. Someone had inscribed on the tarred backside of one of the dilapidated buildings in huge white-wash letters: "EAT SHIT . . . IT'S NON FATTENING."

It was almost two weeks since my last interview, the one with Keating. The one that really counted, and I hadn't heard anything yet. Damn! I was beginning to worry. A fat green fly circled past my ear then buzzed to a stop. I watched him, feeling the urge to smash him, but let it pass.

The waiting was killing me! Soon school would recess for the summer, and the weekly stipend checks from SEEK would end too. Money would start getting tight if I didn't make a move soon. Shit, I could kick myself in the ass for not trying to get another summer job. I just mighta been too sure of myself, depending on CBS.

The screen door on the porch next door swung shut with a soft clack.

"Good morning." It was Alma, my mother-in-law, who lived

25

in the adjoining house. Her deep contralto voice strained through a half-stifled yawn.

"What you doing up so early?"

Early, shit—it was already 10:30!

"I couldn't sleep."

"Couldn't sleep? All that liquor you and Bob drank. He's still dead to the world. Where's Ava?"

"She went down to the meat market a while ago; oughta be back soon." I wondered what she wanted with my wife. Alma always wanted something.

I reached down beside my leg for the half-filled bottle of San'Gria and poured myself another drink. Alma, her big-shit friends, and this stink-ass neighborhood were the main reasons I had to have that job at CBS.

All of Alma's self-important, fart-filled friends had been at the party last night—doctors, lawyers, professors, nurses. All partying their butts off, raising hell just like bona fide niggers! Everyone was having a ball when Alma, feeling good and high, flapped open her mouth: "My son-in-law's going to work for CBS!" I was suddenly swarmed with congratulations.

We all drank a toast to my new career, a career I didn't know if I had yet, but it felt good to be momentarily part of the INNER CROWD. For once Ava really seemed proud of me.

The party conversation then made an abrupt jump from my shining future and landed full force on the back of the lazy, undomesticated, good-for-nothing NIGGER! It was the INNER CROWD's favorite pep talk, and I had heard it many, many times before. Professor Williams took the lead. According to him, it was the nigger's own fault that he was kept down. In fact he kept himself down! He just wasn't shit, and a nigger never tried to be shit. He didn't want to work, and when he did he threw away his money on liquor and women. A nigger left his family so the welfare would take care of them, and the nigger women were just as bad because they would rather have babies and get on welfare than work. A

26

nigger didn't pay his bills and was a fool who blamed the white man for all his troubles. A nigger should be like the white man instead of rioting and burning things down. A nigger should go to school and learn some sense. They, the INNER CROWD, were examples of how good Negroes should behave. Look how much money and education they had! Niggers should get off their asses! They didn't want to be bothered with no niggers. Niggers made them ashamed. Niggers! niggers! NIGGERS!

I got tired of that shit. When Alma's old man, Bob, said he was going upstairs I grabbed a bottle and took off after him, leaving Ava sitting there nodding her head. We sat in his bedroom a long while afterwards drinking and talking about them real stupid NIGGERS downstairs. Bob and I knew that we didn't belong in the INNER CROWD, but our wives did!

That crowd anxiously gulped down huge doses of an elixir brewed from college diplomas, Lenox Terrace apartments, Cadillac cars, and anyone that possessed them. The brew allowed the INNER CROWD to forget that they were niggers. I could not, did not want to, forget.

I wasn't quite two years old when a mob of armed white folks ran my father out of Georgia. They wanted to lynch Dad because he didn't stand there and take it when his boss-man slapped him upside the head. Pop punched him out and hopped a northbound freight train. The bossman was a Klansman!

Pop sent for my mother the next year, and eighteen months later she came back to Georgia for me. We caught a Grey-hound to New York and a subway to Harlem, but we didn't stay in Harlem long. We moved to the Bronx.

Dad lost his job on the Brooklyn docks after a winch slipped and dropped a heavy load on his foot. He always believed it had been meant for his head! We got by then on Dad's Workmen's Compensation check and what Mom brought home—her pay and white folks' leftover food. They once sent me a box of paint-chipped, mostly armless, legless, headless toy soldiers, an eyeless teddy bear, a racing car with three missing wheels, and rough, hand-me-down clothes that made my skin crawl when I wore them to school.

I didn't fuck around in school. Dad gave out ass-kickings for any grade below 75 with the reminder between razor strap blows on my naked ass: "You is a Negro boy; you gotta learn some sense!"

The ass-kickings stopped after Pop got put out. Mom said he was acting like a goddamn nigger, throwing his money away, chasing after women, and not supporting his family. Momma found someone who would, and she remarried two years later.

High school ended with a bang for me. A teacher was blocking the lunchroom exit. I wanted to go out. He said I'd have to go through him. I DID! That put the cops on my trail, so I boosted my age, Mom signed the papers, and I became a U.S. Marine. I was proud to be a Marine, and I met a lot of crackers!

*   *   *

I leaned back in the sunshine flinging my arms up over my head in a long, groaning stretch. About halfway through I heard Ava's muffled footsteps coming down the hall into the kitchen. "Boobie, it's a telegram for you," she called as she stepped out onto the back porch.

Still seated, I turned and took the yellow envelope from her outstretched hand. Ava watched silently as I tore it open and read: "PLEASE REPORT TO MY OFFICE IN THE CBS BUILDING 51 WEST 52ND STREET 25TH FLOOR MONDAY AT 11:30 A M MICHAEL KEATING"

A slow smile crossed my lips. This was it! I looked up at Ava, and she was smiling too.

I got up and went into the kitchen for some ice. I punched out some ice cubes, tossed them into a tall red glass and pushed back out onto the porch. I stood looking down into the yard. Maybe civil rights might be working after all. Maybe

President Johnson's message was finally getting across. He'd admitted on a nationwide broadcast to the whole wide world that it was wrong the way America was treating its black folks. The man had really let it all hang out. I'd heard all that bullshit before, but never from a cracker from Texas.

Then he really got to me, at the end, when he said, "WE SHALL OVERCOME!"

* * *

Like most of the others in that stone and chrome building on the Avenue of the Americas, my office on the twenty-fifth floor was white on black and black on white, giving everyone in it a metallic sheen that reflected itself in the crispness of the men's daily linen and the clickety-tap heels of the women brisking down the halls toward the Xerox room in the center of the floor. No one I knew in that building kept a bottle of whisky in his desk drawer for a warm nip toward the end of the day when someone dropped by.

There usually were only three chairs in my office, mine and two for visitors. There was a desk, a small table upon which sat a green plant—watered once a week by a watering man who came around in a white uniform, and dusted once a month by a dusting man who came around—two prints on the walls selected by people responsible for selecting prints for the walls, and a floor-to-ceiling window that looked westward across Manhattan. Today my secretary brought three other chairs to my office to accommodate the visitors I was waiting for—five young black men and women. My telegram had instructed them to be at my office at 11:30. I was going to tell them that they had been selected as the first participants in the WCBS-TV Journalism Apprenticeship program.

I waited, swinging back in my chair, the only one with a flexible back.

I had met them all before during the series of interviews of the dozen or so minority students sent over to the station by the SEEK program at City College.

Sandra arrived first, right on time, and sat in one of the chairs. I felt immediately at ease with Sandra. She behaved in white, familiar ways. Her parents were mixed, white and black, and Sandra took from the combination a dusky exotica in her appearance—a *café au lait* color, an etched nose, a full mouth, and a tumbling of black curls. She attracted me.

Sandra and I chatted about this and that while I suppressed my impatience and mounting annoyance with the others for being late. For chrissake, they knew it was an important meeting—I had sent those telegrams specifically for that effect—and still they were late! It was going to be difficult dealing with blacks. I could see that.

But I did not want the meeting to begin in a fit of bad temper from me, the leader, about to assume the role of white guardian angel and inspiration to a group of young blacks. I was going to put them into the mainstream of American mass communications, just like that! Lucky them! Lucky me!

At 11:40—ten minutes past the appointed time—the rest of the group arrived en masse, and my moment was at hand, the white liberal's dream come true. I was going to spread joy to a group of underprivileged young blacks.

"Good morning, Jackie. . . . Good morning, Jimmy. . . . Good morning."

"Good morning, Mr. Keating. Good morning."

"Everyone feeling good?" My irritation had subsided. This would be a happy occasion.

"Yeah . . . feeling good."

"Jimmy, why don't you take that seat? . . . Jackie, over here." Everyone was getting settled.

In came Betsy, my secretary. "Anyone like some coffee?" Everyone would, and while we waited the chatter rose in the office, not a lint speck of nervousness on anyone's best clothes.

I savored the moment while the group settled themselves, talking to each other. I wondered how I would make the announcement, speculated as to how good I would feel at their reaction. The whole program seemed like a great idea!

They were trying to slump their bodies into their chairs, but they did not succeed. They remained on the edges, tense and watchful. But not watching me. As I looked around every eye was carefully averted.

After Betty served the coffee and left, I asked Jimmy to close the door. He rose stiffly, his weightlifter muscles bulging incongruously through his narrowcut Madison Avenue suit. Everyone remained silent while he executed the maneuver.

I decided that the best way to impress the importance of the occasion was to be simple.

"Well—" looking around, catching everyone's eye, "I asked you all to come down today to tell you that you have been accepted into the apprenticeship program. The people here will be this year's group. The first . . . Congratulations to all of you."

I smiled broadly, feeling good, and looked around, waiting for the sight, sound, and feel of joy, of elation, of opportunities gained, of new beginnings, new challenges, new lives.

The black faces were blank. No smiles, no exuberance, no stunned looks, no hysteria, no backslaps, no shaking hands with the boss, no nothing. Silence. Jesus Christ, it was weird!

"I assume you all feel good about this," I said, breaking the heavy silence.

"Yeah, it's good," Jackie said unsmilingly. I noticed a smile begin to tease Sandra's mouth, but she caught it before it took hold.

"Any chance of getting more money?" It was Jackie, a nutbrown, shiny, bright-eyed young woman bouyant in her bold Afro chic. Saucy little bitch with a perky bubble of an ass, like a football player's. They were to be paid only $75 a week, and some of them had made it plain in the original interviews that they were unhappy about that.

"I'm continuing to see what I can do about the money. But it doesn't look good." I was pissed at the question. It wasn't time for stuff like that. It was time for celebration, champagne, pats on the back, and gratefulness to Mr. Keating, the white knight who through dint of a lot of pushing, shoving, and long hours had gotten this program started, the one that was giving them access to that dream of Radcliffe girls and young men from Yale—a job as a journalist at CBS! In New York! Mecca!

But there was no display of enthusiasm or even warmth, and certainly no thanks from that strange little group sitting in my office.

"Okay," I said, cutting it short. "You all should see Joan now and she'll fill you in on the personnel procedures. We'll meet next Monday at the CBS cafeteria in Broadcast Center over on West 57th Street. See you then."

The meeting ended. I was bewildered and hurt.

❊　❊　❊

The CBS cafeteria was like a small airline terminal, cool and slick! Inclined ramps led in and out of several sleek entrances busy with people who looked like travelers. Some were carrying little bags slung over their shoulders, while others carried thin aluminum attaché cases in their hands. All types of people brushed past me—young, middle-aged, and some that were almost old but didn't act it. The few black dudes could have been porters.

The new blacks—two girls, two guys—were all sitting together when I entered. They saw me as I came through the entrance, the same time I saw them. We had all met at one time or another in school or during the interview sessions at CBS. They started smiling and waving me over to their table—well, our table. It would have been mighty shitty of me to go and sit somewhere else. Besides, Sandra was at that table—hi yaller, sweet thing. You could taste her she was so fine. A very uppity bitch, though. Lived in Co-op City with the middle classes.

32

Jackie Jones was there too. Nut-brown Afro mama, smart, sensual, dynamite!

Then there was light-skinned, freckle-faced Freddie Cole. He looked so white and felt so black. Smart dude, though. Didn't trust white folks, he said.

Norman Parks, the most sensitive of the group, was a poet with soft, brown, hungry eyes and a cunning smile. He was afraid of his talents and terrified of white people—a tall, quiet, introverted person with pain in his guts.

We all sat around the cafeteria talking while we waited for someone to arrive and tell us what to do next. Between conversations about school, job interviews, and other bullshit, I kept thinking—here I am at CBS. Man, what the fuck is gonna happen next in my life? Might wind up in Hollywood. Shit, move over Sidney, you too Harry, Ossie make some room . . . Why not?

I couldn't help noticing that this place was a whole lot different from the feedpens of PS 99, JHS 40, or Morris High School, where the young people acted like the slop they were given—nasty. They were called cafeterias too, but they were places where you screamed, fought, gouged, bit, and robbed one another like wild cats in a trainer's cage. Places where kids on the free lunch program were fucked over by all the others. Yeah, man, this place was different. Photos of all sizes hung from the wall, scenes of New York and happy people playing, laughing, happy. The whole cafeteria had a happy feeling—pastel walls, shiny chrome, shiny floors, and smiling shiny people who looked like they were out of the magazine section of the newspaper. All that clean happiness got to me. I was happy just to be around so much happiness.

"There's Chris Borgen!" Jackie nudged Freddie sitting next to her, nodding toward the cafeteria entrance where a wavy haired man sat with a blonde woman many shades lighter than him.

It was him all right, Channel Two's star reporter, rapping

to that good looking bitch. His mouth was running a mile a minute and he gestured vigorously with his hands and body. She'd say something and he'd completely relax listening to her. Then he'd start again, fast as ever. Sandra thought he was cute.

"Is he black?"

I wanted to say, "Ask him, BITCH!" but I let the temptation pass. They were the first words she'd spoken to me other than to tell me her name.

"Don't know, baby, but he is dark."

A few more heavies were coming in now—Jim Jensen, dig that name, caught you like Jack Armstrong or Cash McCall. Later we'd call him Diamond Jim. He was the anchorman on the evening news. Bob Potts, another reporter, Frank Gifford, the sportscaster, and others. Our table began to buzz.

"There's so and so. . . . Thought he was taller than that. . . . There's Joan Murray, ain't that sister fine? . . . She ain't so fine to me."

The white folks seated at tables around us were all very polite. Some spoke: "How are yeewww?" Others just nodded and smiled. Some of us nodded and smiled back. They tried hard to pretend that we were nothing unusual, but they were trying too hard.

After we had waited about twenty minutes, a very tall, efficient-looking chick with her hair drawn tightly back into a bun and big round glasses before her eyes whisked through the door, then headed for our table. Her smile began about fifty feet from where I was sitting and by the time she got to the table she was one big happy grin.

"Hi, remember me?" The grin was speaking. "I'm Joan Russell, Mr. Keating's assistant." She sounded happy! "Have you had lunch?"

Some had, some hadn't.

"Well, Mr. Keating is taking us all out to lunch, courtesy of CBS." Then she drew her right hand under her ass to smooth her skirt and sat down. I watched that hand glide

34

over that ass revealing its contours and decided it was kinda flat; not enough cheeks to be interesting.

So Keating was taking us to lunch, huh? Thanks, girl, your boss is a real sport.

"He'll be here in a moment." Damn, she was still showing her teeth. "Mike was delayed. A meeting, you know."

Joan had met us all before when we were interviewed by Mr. Keating. It surprised me that she was able to move right in, calling us by name, making small talk, seeming relaxed, comfortable. I wanted to like her. Caution—wasn't that the prize in Whitey's power bag? That bullshit called personality?

He arrived shortly, The Man himself, the director of the new nigger program, Big Daddy, Mr. Michael Keating! Man, did he come through that entranceway, head held high, shoulders squared, walking erect. You knew he was important. A look of raw intelligence marked his youthful face as he noticed the dark table and started in our direction. The glasses he wore caught the overhead lights, and as he approached us his eyes vanished, becoming reflectors, leaving only a mirrored glare. His was a face created by technology; no smiles, no grins.

"Hi, gang." His voice was dry and flat.

He took a deep breath. "Everyone here?"

No one was missing. Another deep breath. "Good. Hope you're all hungry?"

He smiled: a quick upturn at the corners of his mouth. Joan, looking up at the boss, answered for us.

"Some of the guys have eaten already, but the girls are starved. . . . I'm sure the fellas could eat again."

We could!

We left, Mike, Joan, and Sandra leading the way. Once outside on 57th Street, Mike stopped the procession.

"It's a nice day. . . . Let's walk. Okay?"

The way he spoke it damn shore wasn't a question. It was okay because he said it was okay. He liked making decisions for other people. I was noticing how easy it was for him,

35

how casual, like he wasn't telling you but wanted you to tell yourself—Mr. Keating knows best.

He took off like he wanted to run, Joan right up with him and Sandra keeping pace. The rest of us paired off. We didn't try to keep up.

Halfway up the block Joan looked back and saw that we were far behind. She waited for us, then asked in a musical, little-girl voice: "Is everyone all right?"

"Hell *no!*" Jackie snapped. "Why that man walk so fast?"

"Oh, Mike always walks like that. . . . I have trouble keeping up with him myself, even with my long legs," Joan sighed.

I looked at Joan. The tone Jackie was taking had startled her.

"Maybe he's hungry." I tried a feeble joke to ease the tension.

Joan caught the opening. "He probably is, and can that man eat!" She was glad to change the subject. She was anxious for everyone to smile, laugh, and be happy.

Mike and Sandra were far ahead, jawing their asses off. Dig that bitch trying to make points with Whitey. The half-white motherfucker. I was getting mad. It fucked with my mind when I saw her being so chummy with that white dude Mike. The motherfucker had it all anyway. Shit, big-time sonofabitch, got his choice of ho's, now he want her. Bet if she was as dark as Jackie he wouldn't be strutting so heavy! He couldn't fool me, Baby, with all that respectable horseshit; he wanted to fuck her too! White motherfuckers always want your women. . . . Get her ass on his side and he got control of you. . . . My goddamn mother-in-law for one, always yapping about her fucking white friends, all male, who got money . . . always preaching 'bout the white man is the greatest, nigger men ain't shit nohow. . . . My two daughters were growing up hearing that kinda shit from their grandmother, their mother, and their aunt.

Joan noticed how far ahead Mike and Sandra were and

didn't like it either. Maybe *she* was screwing the boss herself. "You guys don't have to keep up, we're going to 54th and Seventh." She began pulling away from us, calling instructions over her shoulder as she picked up speed. "The restaurant is about midway in the block. We'll all meet there!"

We entered the restaurant and the headwaiter almost fell on his ass rushing over to Mike. A brief conversation and we were led to a back table and seated.

Man! What a place! *Big, dark,* heavy exposed beams crisscrossed overhead, wood paneling covered the walls. Longhaired, pale-skinned couples were grouped at the bar, their asses plopped lazily in bucket-shaped, high-backed stools. More of them sat at tables surrounding us, chewing, drinking, smoking, and talking.

The candles on the table and those around the bar took care of the inside lighting, causing a dimness that sparked my imagination as I dug the mean-looking hand axes, crests, and coats of arms.

Animal heads, mostly steers and rams, hung higher up near the ceiling.

The menus were placed in front of us, and the waiter stood by, pad and pencil in hand. Everything was beef, lamb, or pork—steaks, chops, or roasts. I thought about the animal heads hanging above us, their carcasses devoured long ago. What did they think, forced to look on as jaw after jaw armed with teeth chomped into burnt flesh, tearing it free of bone, crushing that flesh into pulp, then down the gullet to fuel another generation of a fierce species that without mercy forces its victims even in death to witness their destruction, over and over again!

I looked at Mike and Joan scanning their menus. Were they or any of these white people in here different from Whiteys I'd dealt with before? Were they any different from the white teachers in school that disciplined black children by screaming at them, pulling their ears, and then rushing

37

to the sink to scrub away the contact with black skin? Were these people any less fiendish than the ones in the Marine Corps?

"Ah, anyone care for cocktails before we eat?" Mike was looking over his menu calling for everyone's attention. "I'm having a vodka martini." He looked at Sandra on his right. "How about you, Sandra? Like something to drink before you eat?"

Sandra ordered a tom collins or something like that. We all ordered some kinda booze, and the waiter hustled off to the bar.

While we waited for the drinks, Mike began talking about the program. He explained that we each would be assigned to different sections dealing with television journalism and that these assignments would be rotated so that we would quickly get a working knowledge of all assignments and find out what assignments best suited each of us.

Was there a possibility of getting on camera? "Of course," he grinned, "there's a possibility."

Could we expect to have permanent jobs at the end of our training period? "I would think so, but in any case if CBS doesn't keep all of you some other network probably will. You see, as far as I know no other network has set up a training program like this one."

Didn't he know anything for sure? He was the director!

The waiter returned with the drinks. I sat bored to death, listening to the boss do his number, taking a lip trip through his professional and personal adventures. He had finished his vodka martini and was going through his Adventures in Albany Story when our waiter returned. He hesitated a moment while Mike got his punch line in, then with extreme poise excused himself and suggested that we order our food now because of the growing crowd.

Mike got helpful, explaining the food list to us niggers.

"Now some of the dishes are very heavy, some a little lighter. . . . Take the lamb dish. . . . That's lamb chunks

38

dipped in a flour and egg batter and fried in olive oil. . . . Or the Blanquette de Veau."

What the fuck was that? I wondered.

"That's the breast of veal, with carrots, onion, and parsley cooked in butter and served with a sauce."

He went down the list, giving his diagnosis of each dish and whether it matched a mild, medium, or *starving* appetite.

The waiter, every bit the professional in his short red jacket, white shirt, black pants, and bow tie, listened patiently.

"Well, now, do we know what we're going to have?"

The boss looked up from his menu. He seemed pleased with his efforts; the grin on his face was genuine satisfaction. Of course, everyone knew what they wanted; wasn't no nigger at that table dumb enough not to know what he wanted to eat after that meal-by-meal description.

After everyone had ordered, the waiter turned to Mike.

"Will you have wine with your meal?"

"Aaaah, yes."

The reply was quickly followed by a seductive French melody coming from Mike's lips that named the wine. No shit about it, the boss could do that thing, man, precise as Clifton Webb and a little daring, like Paul Newman. They'd be seated with some fine bitch, and when they ordered the wine, the year and name in French, the camera would switch to Doris Day or Joanne Woodward getting hot in the ass or in Miss Woodward's case coming all over herself.

Mike had experienced more than just movies. This was his life, he was doing what came naturally. He was also doing it for the women, trying to make the rest of us males at the table look like shit, doing it mostly for Sandra.

"And bring another round of drinks."

Almost as a second thought, Mike turned to the rest of us: "Is that all right?"

Another round of drinks was all right.

39

The boss was being casual about it, as though he didn't know that the farthest downtown poor niggers came to eat was Wells on Seventh Avenue or Franks on 125th Street. Shit, this place we were in was far south of the Pig Foot and Potato Salad Line!

3 The parallels were constantly asserting themselves—two bottles bobbing in the same tidal flow, carrying separate messages. Sam and I had met in Albany when I was a legislative correspondent for the Associated Press covering the state government and he was counsel to the Assembly Majority Leader.

When I moved to New York with the *Herald Tribune,* he moved to New York to help elect John Lindsay mayor. I went to CBS and became a high-profile citizen of the town; he became a commissioner in the city government when Lindsay won election. I sometimes envied him his jobs, he sometimes envied me mine. Our children were approximately the same ages, although I had four and he had two. Even our wives looked similar; blonde and cool. Sometimes his independence struggles with his wife were much the same as mine with mine.

Sam was on the phone. "Let's have a drink tonight."

"Yeah. Let's do that. Why don't you come by the studio around five and pick me up? You can watch the taping and we can leave from there."

We shared that too, enjoying hours in a comfortable bar,

drinking and arguing, heartening the evening along into a boozy male bonhomie. Simple and refreshing.

By 4 o'clock my work for the day was done—the evening's editorial was written, the general manager had approved it, the script had been sent across town to Broadcast Center to be typed in inch-high letters and placed on the Teleprompter, waiting for my arrival in the studio at 5 P.M., when I would read my words unrolling on the prompter just above the lens, creating the illusion of direct eye contact between the speaker and the viewer, a personal communication, powerful and intimate.

There was time for a brisk walk from my office in Black Rock at 52d and Sixth to Broadcast Center at 57th and Tenth, a route I traveled rain and shine. By now I knew all the 57th Street regulars by sight—the duck walk of the young ballet dancers heading for the rehearsal halls, the tailored, expensive hookers, the few tenement people who had escaped eviction for high-rises sitting on their stoops.

Strangers said hello as I moved quickly along, trying not to notice everyone who noticed me so that I could have some privacy with my thoughts. It was my daily physical exercise and meditation.

Monday through Friday I walked 57th Street for the 5 P.M. taping of that evening's editorial; a continuing rhythm day after day, beginning when I woke in the morning and mounting to the climax of the daily taping. Day after day, in and out like the tide. Some days its regularity was crushing.

Sam Kearing was waiting when I arrived, and the two of us walked through the complex of Broadcast Center corridors to Studio 46. The director and crew were standing by, waiting until the technican at central control turned on Studio 46 at precisely 5 P.M.

At 4:50, in the darkened studio, I sat down at my plywood desk, isolated in a lone pool of light, hearing but not seeing the quiet shuffling of the handful of technicians work-

42

ing in the dark outside my bright aura. I arranged my tie, smoothed my hair, pulled the back of my jacket under my ass to keep it from bunching behind my neck when I leaned into the camera, and offered my face to the makeup lady.

It was psyche-up time, and I withdrew into myself, curling my tongue and pressing it against the roof of my mouth, stretching its muscles so enunciation would be vigorous and crisp, closing my mind to all thoughts other than the lens in front of me, personalizing that little circle of blue-purple glass on the camera so that it became the collected psyches of the hundreds of thousands of people I was about to address, directly, one to one, eyeball to eyeball, telling them how I, the spokesman for the management of WCBS-TV, thought the country should be run, forgetting about Sam watching me on the monitor in the control room, waiting for us to have our drink and talk.

The red light below the lens flicked to a glow, and I began to read my words, concentrating on the meaning of each as my tongue put it together. In 2 minutes, 57 seconds it was over. The first take was good. We left the building.

"You were strange after the taping." Sam and I were alongside each other on heavy leather stools, leaning inward over the burnished wood of the Berkshire Hotel bar on Madison Avenue.

"Strange?"

"Yeah. You seemed so high, so distant. When you came into the control room after you were done you looked right through me. You were some place else, like you didn't know where you were."

Yes, that was the feeling, although I hadn't recognized it before Sam brought it to my notice.

Yes, I had surrendered a little piece of myself to that videotape—I sensed that now—and each taping left a hole in me that needed refilling. Now, with drinks in our hands in the comfortable bar, the day over, I could feel myself touching ground, returning. Refilling.

43

"I hadn't realized I was that way after a broadcast."

"You hadn't? Well, you'd better calm down, Keating. You're getting too wrapped up in it." It was one of Sam's favorite constructions when we went out together. I was taking myself too seriously, getting pompous and humorless, while he floated about city government, laughing and plucking flowers. He was, in fact, a compulsive hard worker and flashily energetic.

"There's not much to be done about that, Sam. That's the nature of the business. I mean you just can't sit there in front of the camera and start talking and expect people to be interested just because your lips are moving. You've got to get into it—you've got to believe your own words. Television is too intimate for deception, at least too intimate for constant deception, night after night. The viewer will catch on eventually, and he'll stop watching. You've got to be up for it and believe in it, all the time."

"Bullshit!"

We smiled fondly at one another and ordered another drink. Sam loved media, particularly television.

"I think you've got one of the great jobs—sitting there every night telling everybody what to do. A pompous guy like you. You gotta love it! A television personality! Christ, don't you think that's a lot better than busting your ass chasing down ten stories a day for the AP and getting paid peanuts?"

"No, no, don't get me wrong. The job seems fine. The money's pretty good. I'm getting what I want; the General Managers don't hassle me too much. But—"

"But? But what?"

But what? There was a gnawing going on inside, a not quite realized sense that a conviction was forming within, a conviction that when it emerged into the consciousness would be a self-judgment that would be trouble for me. I suspected that the judgment would be that the life I was taking so seriously was a charade.

44

Well, that was nothing I could articulate at the moment. It would be foolish to startle Sam with such a thought and then be unable to explain it further. I could only speak of the parts, not the conclusion that I felt developing.

"The hatred, Sam. The hatred gets me down sometimes."

"Hatred? What do you mean?"

I told him of the telephone calls after an editorial broadcast, some of them useful, nearly all of them interesting in some way, not all of them pleasant. Most of them were not. Calls from cops, firemen, taxi drivers, teachers, businessmen, wives, gamblers, bus drivers, politicians, horny women, and various eccentrics. Sometimes five calls after an evening editorial, sometimes three hundred, depending on how excited people became at the subject and the message. The nightly phone calls were an instant barometer of how the half-million viewers I talked to each night felt about the public issues.

The race hatred. The number of calls was always high after an editorial that dealt with any of those favorite devices that were to give blacks an equal taste of the cornucopia—open housing, school integration, job equality. Oh yes, the phone buttons would light up after one of those editorials where I took the liberal position. Rasping white voices shouting "nigger lover! How can you support these animals? . . . Do you see the way they live throwing garbage on the streets? . . . Nigger. . . . Coon." And also the smooth voices asking with grating snideness: "And where do your children go to school, Mr. Keating? Do they go to school with those people you seem to love so much? Where do you live, Mr. Keating? I'm sure you live up there in Connecticut with all the nice people, don't you, Mr. Keating?"

"I've stopped staying and answering my own phone, Sam. I can't stand it any more. Ugly."

The bartender stopped by and gave us two more scotches.

"And one of the bedeviling aspects of it all, Sam, is these

45

guys who call up and say: 'And how many colored people do you have at CBS, Mr. Keating?'

"I want to shout out to those bastards—Fuck you, you racist pig! But you and I know, Sam, that there are just about zero blacks at CBS."

"I haven't seen any," he said.

"Oh, there are a few here and there. We have meetings every now and again and everyone describes how strenuously he's trying to find qualified blacks. But no one seems to find any."

"More bullshit," Sam said. "That crowd at CBS wants to make a buck, that's all. All the rest of the CBS image is fake. Look at the shit they put on the air. You think they care? C'mon Mike. You gotta be a believer to do the job? Is that your problem?"

Well, that was it, more or less. Yes, goddam right. I had to believe. I had been a journalist since I was eight years old, hand-printing carbon copies of a family newspaper that I sold to the cousins, in-laws, and other relatives gathered at the Christmas table. Goddamn right! My work had to have nobility, truth, dignity. I wasn't just making a buck; I was doing my bit for society. I wasn't cursing darknesses. I was lighting candles.

If CBS had no function other than making money for the chairman and the other stockholders, then fuck it. If CBS wasn't serious about telling the story of America and its people, but was interested only in keeping its owners wallowing fat, then I was in a deep personal dilemma.

Yes, I felt the conviction take a little further jump forward toward my consciousness, like the gum twinge of an incoming wisdom tooth.

Sam was laughing, and I was getting irritated.

"Don't patronize me, Kearing, or I'm gonna get pissed. You're no different than I am. You think John Lindsay's going to save America, so don't play the cynic with me."

We both laughed and had another round.

46

"Things seem to be changing at CBS, Sam. Tightening. I'm getting criticisms now from upstairs. It's the first time."

"Yeah? What's been happening?"

"Well, for instance, I have never heard from William Paley vis-à-vis editorial positions. Company policy says very definitely that editorial positions are the responsibility of the general managers and editorial boards of each CBS station—no pronouncements from on high. That's been the practice.

"But the other day the General Manager stops by and leaves this file of memos on my desk. The first memo was a query from Paley to the company's economist. Paley wanted to know what he thought of one of my editorials supporting Bobby Kennedy's efforts to tighten up the tax laws so there wouldn't be so many loopholes for the rich."

"Like Paley," Sam interjected.

"Yeah, like Paley. Well, the economist, of course, thought the editorial was really stupid, you know. He said it showed no understanding of the complexities of the tax laws, and even the word 'loophole' that I had used was a naïve, even irresponsible word. That memo was in the packet.

"Then there was another memo from some other Ph.D. on Paley's staff, saying more of the same, and others contributed their bit as the memos went down the line toward me, accumulating size like a snowball.

"And they all assured the chairman that his tax loopholes were, in the long, responsible view, the best thing for the country. Editorialist Keating obviously had been sucked into another one of Bobby Kennedy's base maneuvers for votes from the unthinking, and let's hope Keating does his homework better and wises up. That sort of stuff.

"The whole piece of shit was dumped on my desk, all stapled together."

"What did you do?" Sam asked.

"Well, I was really pissed—all those ass-kissers trying to pass off their ass-kissing as superior knowledge and expertise. It had never happened to me before, and I've been doing

47

these editorials for a few years now. I was really mad, but, oh, I went through the motions. I spent a whole week composing a memo in response, quoting all the tax authorities, arguing the anti-loophole case, and all that. And I delivered the memo to the General Manager for passage up the pipeline to Paley. Maybe he did send it on. I don't know. I don't expect him to, and I won't ask. And I'll keep suggesting that we do other editorials against tax loopholes—it's a big issue —but I know he won't allow them on the air.

"I mean, we're grown up. The General Manager knows what that packet of memos was telling him. I know too. Paley owns the company. Period."

"And that local autonomy is bullshit, then?" Sam asked.

"I never used to think so, but it's looking that way now. Something seems to be happening within the company. I'm getting the feeling that they're finding me intolerable."

"With good reason, Keating!" and we both laughed and had another drink, moving our talk into gossip and girls, making a night of it, savoring the level of communication.

A man disengaged himself from the bar at the end where it touched the wall, put on his coat, picked up his paper, and walked toward the door. He would pass us en route.

As he came behind us, he inserted his groomed head between ours, put his arm around my shoulder, and said in Connecticut tones:

"Don't listen to this guy, Michael. I want you to know I'm with you all the way. I think you're doing a great job."

The breath went out of my lungs as I smiled weakly at him, supposedly grateful for his attention. The bastard had been eavesdropping on our entire conversation!

Jesus! Was there no escape? I felt more and more of my life being taken over by my job. The areas of my privacy were getting narrower and narrower. I was overcome then with the sense of becoming a talking machine turned on at 5 P.M., Monday through Friday, rain and shine, then put on display for the rest of the time, always ready with an intelligent opinion when the right button was pushed.

And what was the connection between my reality, CBS's, and the words that came out when the button was pushed?

*　*　*

It was in the '50s, in the Ambassador Restaurant across State Street from the Capitol in Albany. A young black assistant to Governor Rockefeller started talking too much, as he often did after a few drinks.

He turned to us—four legislative correspondents—and began a critique of the "white press." It was ignoring the reality of black life in America, he said.

White press? "What do you mean 'white press'?" I asked. I had never heard the term before.

"I mean white press—the press produced by white men for white readers."

"That's crap," I said. "The press is the press—for everybody. There's the general press and the special-interest press, like the ethnic papers and the racial papers, such as the *Amsterdam News*. There's no such thing as the white press. When I report a story I report it for everybody, not just white people."

His words stayed with me, and when I moved to New York and saw the multitude of black faces in the streets and the scarcity of them in the studios and the newsrooms in which I worked, I began to wonder about the words of the man in Albany.

I had become friendly with Layhmond Robinson, a reporter on the *New York Times* and one of the few black reporters in the country at the time. He only discussed the matter when asked, and eventually I asked him.

Yes, he told me, there is a white press and I am it.

When the blacks rioted in the cities in the '60s, no one needed to prove the point any more that when it came to black news it was seen with white eyes, and the difference in color produced differences in the "facts."

"The media report and write from the standpoint of a white

49

man's world," concluded the National Advisory Commission on Civil Disorders. It used the term—"white press."

Those reporters and camera crews who had attempted to cover the riots had discovered their white isolation when they entered the black communities. There they were greeted not as celebrities and keepers of the keys to the media that they considered themselves, but as liars and an integral part of the white oppression. They discovered that there were large areas of their cities where they could not perform their job of reporting because few people would trust them, and others threatened their lives and drove them out. Metropolitan newspaper, television, and radio reporters and editors discovered their ignorance of large sections of their own communities.

As Editorial Director of WCBS-TV I had no direct connection with the station's news coverage of the riots and the aftermath of bitterness. I sympathized with the abuses my white colleagues suffered on the streets, but at the same time I believed they—we—deserved it. The white arrogance that I had only recently discovered in my profession deserved the rap. That's what I believed. It was not what I said. I could not bring myself to say it on the air or in meetings of the Editorial Board. It would have been too outrageous.

It came out in other ways.

As a result of the report of the national commission criticizing the white complexion and white bias of the broadcast and print media, CBS as a corporation became interested in numbers—how many minorities did this and that department add last month? The pressure was on, and at WCBS-TV discussions about the minority hiring problem became numerous and serious.

So when the scramble began to find black faces to put on television, I knew that something more could be done, that the putting forth of black faces would result in only a cosmetic change, that the issue was not merely black visibility on the tube, but also black substance in the reporting.

Let's seize the occasion to add black attitudes as well as

black faces to the Channel Two news image, I argued at the station meetings. I suggested we search out and hire not the few well-to-do sons and daughters of the black bourgeoisie who would share the same attitudes as the white ruling class, but ghetto youths who were fiery and angry about their oppression, who would understand the street experience, and who would be more representative of the black population in our area. They would make the strongest journalists, I felt, and could bring to television news the attitudes, styles, anger, vigor, and even language of the black inner city, thereby exposing the whites in our audience to a reality they lived beside but never saw. They could also provide the large black audience, particularly the younger audience, with people and stories they could relate to. And as the audience surveys showed, blacks were the most faithful TV audience. They loved TV. Did we love them?

My ideas were accepted. I was appointed to design a program to accomplish the goal, and to run it.

So now my suggestions, vaguely romantic as they were, had to be made into programs. Where to find the candidates?

Ah, yes. Where did one find trained journalists who looked, spoke, and behaved black and militant?

They did not exist in any identifiable numbers. No newsroom would have them, and they were not in the journalism schools. We would have to find our own.

For a week or two I discussed the problem regularly with my staff. My assistant came into my office one morning with a copy of *The Nation* in his hand.

"Interesting article here, Mike. Might give you some ideas about the apprenticeship program." He dropped the magazine on my desk.

The article, written by an assistant professor at the City College of New York, described the author's experiences teaching English to a group of students taken into college directly from New York City's ghettos. The students, basically black and Puerto Rican, would not ordinarily have been admitted to the college. Under the special program, they were given special courses, psychological counseling, and financial help. The author said the results were one of the few hopeful signs that he knew of in higher education.

The program at City College seemed to me to be parallel to what we had in mind at WCBS-TV: bypassing the traditional routes in order to accomplish a specific end—that is, bringing minorities into the white mainstream.

If we could hook up with City College, we could draw our candidates from their enrollment, thereby eliminating for us the elaborate work of identifying potential participants and recruiting them. A stroke of luck! A quick and easy start on our new program.

The author of the article was Leonard Kriegel, a man I happened to have met a year or two before when he had struggled into the CBS Broadcast Center on his crutches, dragging his crippled legs, to deliver on the air a rebuttal to an editorial I had delivered supporting Mayor Lindsay's crackdown on illegally parked cars, including those of the disabled.

I called him the day after reading the article. He arranged a meeting with the director of the program, and after a few weeks of discussion we agreed to operate the station's apprenticeship program in conjunction with the City College's pre-Baccalaureate program, called SEEK. They sent us a group of candidates, and we selected five from them to begin the program—three males, two females, all black.

Two days before Robert Kennedy was assassinated in Los Angeles in 1968, the five apprentices began work for the summer at WCBS-TV. They were assigned to fixed periods of time in three departments of the station: news, program, and my own editorial department. The structure was such that at the end of the summer all of the students would have experienced all of the station's broadcast activities.

After the chill of the initial meeting in my office with the five apprentices, I knew that communication with them would be difficult. I sensed their suspicion and, while hurt

52

by it, respected them for having it. After all, I was having my own suspicions about CBS and what I was doing.

To maintain contact with them throughout the summer while they performed jobs in various parts of the station, I met them for lunch each Friday noon in the CBS cafeteria. My hope was that we would discuss experiences, resolve problems, answer questions, and keep enthusiasm high.

"How do you like it where you are, Jackie?" I asked.

"Oh, I like working with the people." She put down her sandwich and reached for a Coke. "But the work is boring —logging in all that crap. I want to go out with the camera crews or work on a documentary."

"Well, that'll come. You're up there now so you'll get an idea of how the over-all station works. It won't be long. Everyone will get a turn at everything. And you, Jimmy, how's it going?"

Jimmy Watson looked up from his overloaded plate—the man ate like a horse. "Everything's going fine. Everything's okay. I'm just anxious to get working with the Eye on New York unit."

"And you, Freddie?"

"Okay."

"Norman?"

"Fine."

The luncheons went on that way, going nowhere. They were determined to tell me nothing, to operate on their own, no matter how slyly I tried to draw them out. I did not like the rebuff, and I was jealous to maintain control of the program. It was mine.

Eventually we stopped having lunch together.

The only complaint they would discuss with me with any openness was the pay. The $75 a week left them unhappy, and I had been unsuccessful in trying to raise it. It was the union wage for beginners in the nontechnical side of television.

"Look," I told them after about the sixth complaint, "what

you are being paid is what all the desk assistants are paid. The union will not allow you people to be paid more than their own members. You gotta remember that the unions agreed to waive the usual requirements in order to get you people in these jobs in the first place."

"Unions. They're always fucking us." It was Jackie again, pushing. "How you expect us to get along on $75 a week?"

"Everyone else seems to be able to do it. There are people here from the best colleges in the country taking that kind of money. And if they don't want to take it there's a lineup stretching to the West Coast of people who would love to have these jobs. Because this is New York and CBS. You've got to understand that. We pay you more than the rest and the whole newsroom would be disrupted."

They did not like that speech, but they did not argue further that day.

There were other problems, all of which I learned of from people outside the apprenticeship program.

Although I had been in and out of the newsroom daily for a couple of years, I had not been aware of the open and foul-mouthed racial bigotry there, particularly among some of the camera crews—people who were protected by strong, lily-white unions in which the well-paying jobs of cameraman, soundman, and electrician were passed from father to son, uncle to cousin, and business agent to son-in-law, jobs impossible to lose even though a few of the cameramen had difficulty shooting in focus. "Nigger . . . coon . . . black bastard" peppered the daily speech of some of them regardless of whether a black ear was within range. Their continual run-ins with hostile blacks and Puerto Ricans while covering tense stories in the city's ghettos increased their hostility.

The apprentices were hurting, I was told. I had to find some way to determine what was going on with them. They would not tell me, so I asked all of them to write me an essay dealing with their experience at CBS and their opinions of the apprenticeship program. The only response came from Norman Parks, a sensitive twenty-year-old man who was dealing with white people for the first time despite having spent his entire life in what we used to believe was the New York melting pot. He wrote:

"Keating said that he'd heard from various sources that I was having problems of a 'racial aspect.' I thought that this man had a lot of nerve asking me that question. I thought, shit, he's just like the rest of them. . . . I was having problems of a 'racial aspect.' Well, Keating was right.

"I don't know when it started or maybe it didn't start at all. A man from Graphics called Jimmy Watson an orangutan. Yeah, that's when it started. Because I remember how angry Jimmy was. He went right up to that man and he said, 'You gon' call me an orangutan!' and the man said 'What?' and Jimmy weighing about 200 pounds of nothing but muscle had a few more words with him. The man was so scared he almost turned black himself. I was glad that Jimmy did what he did because I would have been scared to do it myself.

"After this incident I became very uneasy around the people in the office because of other comments I heard. They weren't all cutting statements, but statements made out of ignorance. Statements like 'Where's the colored boy who was around yesterday?' and 'The colored boy over there has the lineups.'

"Sometimes the desk assistants would indulge in conversation about their trips to Europe, and I would try to get in on the conversation. But they knew that not many Niggers get to go to faraway places and the only faraway place that I had been was California and that was to help some brothers riot in Watts. I know that they sensed that I wanted to conversate, but by the time they sensed it I didn't want to talk anyway. I felt invisible."

There was little I could do to help. I did not want to post a sign in the newsroom saying love your fellow man regardless of race, creed, or color. I took Norman Parks aside and told him I understood, that I could do little for him other than to offer him my respect and my understanding, and my advice. I told him that bigotry was a fact of life with the

55

white man, that as a black he would be dealing with that fact all his life as long as he stayed in the white man's television, or in any activity dominated by the white man. Better start learning now to cope with it.

My advice did not seem to be helpful. Norman was wilting visibly under the pressure. The others appeared not to be bothered as much, as far as I knew. I sought out Jimmy Watson to ask his advice. He was older than the others, seemed stronger, more assured. What did he think was going on with the others?

"I think everything is cool, Mike. No problems. We'd all like a little more scratch. But otherwise okay." He smiled.

I looked at him sharply, letting him know I knew he was bullshitting. But the wall remained impregnable. I noticed, though, that he liked my seeking him out that way.

The apprentices were having problems not only from the white racists in the station. They were making life difficult for each other.

Sandra, the most beautiful of the lot, the one with the most potential for on-the-air news glamour, had become distant, silent, and morose—a radical change. I called her into my office. What was wrong?

For ten minutes we talked of this and that, everything but the answer to the question. Then her eyes misted and she opened:

"I don't know where I fit in. Some of the kids are coming down on me, saying I'm not black. They're saying I'm hungry for the white world because my mother is white. Everytime I say anything, the rest of them jump me."

I had noticed, had felt, the way the apprentices policed each other, keeping on each other a hard, questioning eye for signs of Whitey talk, Whitey thought, Whitey behavior. When they found it, they derided it.

It placed them in double jeopardy—the sneers and disdain of the white racists on the one side, the razor-angry and sometimes paranoid judgments of their black peers on the other. Not a comfortable place to be at eighteen, nineteen, or twenty, an age when even the most secure of us are troubled by our ignorance of who we are.

And who were they? Were they not just the typical ambitious young people trying to make a career for themselves, trying to grab off one of the lucrative jobs that TV abounds in, once you serve your $75-a-week time? Wouldn't they click their heels like everyone else when the big offer was made? Did they really mean what they said about being black and proud and beautiful, or were they merely swimming with the new current, being chic?

After the apprenticeship program was well under way, some of the executives at the station thought it would be a good idea to build a half-hour discussion show around the apprentices and other students from the SEEK program at City College. It would fulfill FCC requirements for public service broadcasting and also provide a little publicity for CBS's noble enterprise in integrated broadcasting.

Based on some other events that had occurred that summer, I knew what one of the first questions would be when the time came to select participants in the show. Would they shave their beards and Afros and look a little less menacing to the white folk? After all, the apprentices would be identified as working for CBS.

I knew I would be asked, and I wanted to say no. But first I had to determine if my no would in fact express the attitudes of the apprentices. I didn't want to be in the position of saying no, then find out that they were asked afterward and said yes.

I stopped Jimmy Watson casually when we passed each other in the corridor.

"Jimmy, how do you feel about your beard? Would you consider shaving it off if something came up that would give you an opportunity to go on the air."

His eyes hooded. "Why do you ask that?"

"Oh, I just want to know should the question arise."

He thought for a moment. "No, I wouldn't."

57

4 I'd hiked all the way crosstown and was standing, sweating my nuts off, looking at the entrance of a long, squat building with a big 'EYE' staring out from its red brick wall when a cute swinging miniskirt led me inside to begin my first day on the job, an assistant on the traffic desk at WCBS-TV News.

I bounced up a short flight of stairs. The skirt turned right and I turned left, stepping into a short lobby. A few feet away there was an entrance with a bigger than life photo on each side—Frank Gifford to the right, Jim Jensen to the left.

Yeah, man, I thought, this must be the place—the WCBS-TV newsroom. I hustled between the two grinning faces and turned right, entering a broad, square room divided by a narrow aisle. On one side of the aisle, the wide side, a jumble of people sat machine-gunning typewriters behind short, tight desks cramped with phones and papers. On the narrower side, a short redhead was feeding a noisy, chewing Xerox machine pushed next to a half-filled water cooler. To the rear, at the end of the aisle, the room was cut up into small cubicles like an ice tray with a head or two sticking up.

I eased over to the pint-sized redhead. "Where's Elmer Reed?"

"At the Traffic Desk." She stuck out her arm, directing me to the corner of the wide side where a little man sat with his back to me looking up at a long, chalk-marked blackboard.

I headed toward him hearing screaming phones, jabbering voices, and clacking typewriters.

Elmer Reed still had his eyes fixed on the blackboard as I strode up to his desk. "Mister Reed!"

He twirled around, facing me with a dumb look on his face. I made my speech:

"Mr. Reed, I'm Jimmy Watson. Mr. Keating sent me over."

"Glad to meetcha. Welcome aboard!" He smiled, looking like a possum, and stuck out his hand. I squeezed it and let it go. He patted the cushioned chair beside him. "Have a seat. Frankie'll show you what to do when he gets back. Just now went to get coffee."

I dropped down and he went back to his board like he was watching for God.

Well, I thought, looking around me, listening to the phones, voices, teletypes, here I am.

I wished my mother could see me now. Always sayin' I wasn't shit . . . probably wind up in the pen somewhere.

A sharp-faced dude popped up, interrupting my thoughts. His long blond hair fell to his eyes as he stood over me with a "What the fuck you doing here?" attitude. Just then, Elmer left his vigil at the blackboard and swiveled around. "Frank, this is the new DA (desk assistant). Jimmy, meet Frank." Frank gave his head a little jerk, tossing the hair from his eyes, said "Hi," and walked off to find another chair. He had just pushed his chair next to mine and was about to sit down when an avalanche of flat circular cans crashed on the desk. A large, ruddy man connected to a huge black handlebar mustache spoke down in a British accent: "These are the films of that fire, 350 feet color, 200 feet black and white," and moved on.

Frank scooped up the film containers, looked at me, and said "C'mon." I got up and followed him to the blackboard, where we spent the next five minutes.

The blackboard was divided into seven sections that listed the story, title, reporter, cameraman, film footage, black and white or color, the date, time received. After we'd chalked in all the necessary information, we stacked the containers and carried them up a dim flight of stairs and through a door marked "Film Lab," and handed them to a dude dressed like a doctor sitting on a small metal table. He slid over and dropped the containers at his side with a soft clank.

"Anything else down there?" He was speaking to Frank but looking at me. Frank said no and was turning to leave when the technician bounced from the table saying, "Hey, wait. Take this!" He reached up and took a container from the top of the film processor and shoved it to me. "Here, take this—" he was looking at Frank and speaking to me. "—with you." Was this motherfucker trying to tell me something? I took the container and followed Frank out the door.

At first it didn't seem too bad being a desk assistant. I'd learned how to log the blackboard, log the equipment, answer the phone. That I liked, answering the phone. Made me feel kinda important, like I really belonged! It was dynamite to pick up and say: "WCBS-TV Newsroom. Desk assistant Jimmy Watson speaking." The person on the other end would tell me who they wanted and I'd shout out: "Dick Lobo," or whoever they wanted, "pick up on five." Now that was real hot shit! The caller didn't always want to speak to a honcho, though. Sometimes they just wanted some information that I could supply or could get for them. But sometimes a jive motherfucker would catch my heavy voice and want to fuck with me. They'd either hang up, in which case I'd be right there waiting for them when they called back, that is if another DA didn't pick up first, or they acted right and said why they'd called. Or they'd get shitty like, "Since

60

when did CBS start teaching coons to answer phones?" I'd
be cool though, not wanting to blow this big-time job, so
I'd say something like, "Since they taught them to talk!
Now can I help you?" That didn't always work. Sometimes
they'd want to get *real* shitty, talking about, "Eh, Sambo,
how many niggers they got down there?" or "Any nigger
pussy down there I could screw?"

I only had one answer for them: "YEAH, ONE, YO'
MOMMA!" But that kind of call didn't come too often.
Most of the calls were from reporters or big-time people
who knew how to act on the phone—like Barry Gottehrer,
assistant to Mayor Lindsay. That call really impressed me.
Talked real cool, like a gentleman. When he asked me was I
black my tongue caught in my teeth. I finally said yes. He
wished me good luck and hung up.

There was a lot of traffic past the Traffic Desk. It seemed
like everyone working in the newsroom, and some who
didn't, just had to stroll by giving me the once-over. I sat
and sized them up too! Especially the broads! About every
twenty minutes, a fine motherfucker with bobbed blonde
hair, a Greek-goddess face and an inverted-heart-shaped ass
would sweep around a little bend, glide past the Traffic
Desk, swish up the narrow aisle, and disappear through the
entrance. I began to watch for her. No matter what I was doing, I'd look up, check the big clock above the blackboard,
and every twenty minutes I'd turn into Pavlov's dog.

She hadn't long vanished through the entrance, leaving a
scented trail that smelled sweet enough to eat, when the
phone rang. I answered in my usual style! It wasn't nothing
much, just a reporter wanting some schedule information.
While I was giving it, a sack of a man eating a pipe drifted
over, stopped and stood over me, sending up smoke signals
like an Indian. He kept fouling the air until I hung up. Then
he snatched the pipe from his mouth and offered his hand.
I grabbed it.

"You're new here, aren't you? I'm Walter Arm," and he
kept on talking.

61

As I was nodding yes and pumping his hand, I spied Aphrodite coming back down the aisle. I kept watching her and pumping him while she kept on getting closer. A few steps away she gave me a smile. Instinctively I smiled back, still jerking on Walter's arm. For an instant, she was partially hidden crossing behind his back but my head was following her like radar, my arm still pumping the juice. As she stepped past him, she puckered her lips and pushed me a silent kiss. I pushed one back and the sweet young lady dipped around the bend.

Walter looked to his right, still engaged to my hand, but evidently he'd missed her. His head snapped back around. He stared down at me with a puzzled expression. Then he unfastened his hand and walked away, shaking his head and sending up smoke signals. Much later I learned he was the City Editor. Not long after Walter walked away, Frankie tapped my shoulder. "It's time for lunch."

After I'd stuffed myself in the cafeteria, I hurried back to the newsroom. I'd taken too much time eating and was running late. I plodded up to the traffic desk. Frankie was waiting. "I wanna show ya another part of ya' job."

He led me to a room a little bit smaller than a good-sized outhouse. A loud, quick-tapping noise was coming from a row of beatle-shaped machines sitting on a narrow metal bench. The machines spewed from their mouths a printed trail of paper that hung down to the floor and under the bench.

"This," Frankie said, moving his arm in a tight semicircle, "is the wire room."

He then gave me a blow-by-blow description of what I was to do in the wire room, ending with: "Now, if any machines start to ring like BING! BING! BING! you know it's a bulletin. Get that over to Walter or Dick or somebody quick! Now you got everything?"

I said I had and he left. I browsed around a while reading the news stories the teletype machines chopped out, then I walked out.

Chris Borgen was seated across the aisle from the Traffic Desk punching on a typewriter when I got back. I plopped down and watched him. Chris looked up a moment, saw me gawking, shot me a quick wink and a fast smile, and went back to his punching. It was done in a flash. I didn't have a chance to shoot back! Well, RIGHT ON, BROTHER! You got it made. I said it soft, under my breath, thinking all the while: Gonna be right UP THERE WITH YOU!

I was over by the water cooler an hour or so later getting a drink. I turned and there was Jim Jensen, the anchorman, Man, he walked like he was fucking the Queen. Sharp as a musketeer's peter! His three-piece gray suit looked like IT paid taxes on itself! He swaggered up, looked down at me and said, "Hi, kiddo!" and kept on going. Now where the fuck did he get that "kiddo" shit from? My hot eyes followed him into one of the cubicles in the rear. I hoped the Queen gave him the clap!

In the middle of the thought, a soft, deep voice said, "Excuse me." I rotated my head slowly over my shoulder and blinked up into Frank Gifford's smiling face. I did a quick sidestep to let him go past. He didn't move.

"How much you press?" he asked, still smiling. Now that I liked—somebody realizing that I did something besides run errands and answer phones.

"About two-ninety," I lied, adding on about fifteen pounds.

"I'll stop around and see you sometime; maybe we could go for a workout." He padded away looking like I imagined Jack Armstrong would look—the All-American Man! I felt about two feet taller as I strutted back to the Traffic Desk. Dig that shit! All-American, ex-Giant football star Frank Gifford wanted to work out with ME! I was sorry I'd lied. He came on too straight. Well, I might have those fifteen pounds by the time he was ready.

As the afternoon wore on, I tired of answering phones and running up to the Film Lab, especially the Film Lab. Something about that mole faced dude up there I didn't like. Oh, he never said anything right out, but what he did say didn't sound quite right! Well, fuck him. I wasn't going to be doing this long. This shit was just temporary, Keating had said. Told me that I'd be working on the "Eye on New York" program, the station's weekly documentary, in a day or so. Now that sounded BIG!

Elmer had gone home early and Frankie was in another part of the building when Jackie dropped by during a lull that afternoon. I was glad to see her.

"Hey, Baby! How's it going upstairs in Programing?"

"IT AIN'T!" She dropped down in Frankie's chair, folding one leg over the other. "I'm bored silly . . . sitting up there watching TV programs . . . timing 'em with a stop watch . . . I swear, it's about to drive me nuts. How you making out?"

I told her about my DA's job.

"Hummph! Didn't they say they was going to train us as journalists?"

I didn't answer. I was looking past her. The boss man, Mike Keating, was parading down the narrow aisle. He wasn't alone. Sandra was a pace or two behind—she had been assigned to his office—trained already, just the correct distance away.

Mike swung up to Jackie and me, took a deep breath and said, "Hi, gang, how's everything going?"

We answered in unison, flashing all our front teeth: "Fine." Sandra stood a little to his right looking beautifully dumb. Mike stared down through his glasses like he wanted to take us home to play with his kids. Jackie and me gazed up as if we wanted to go.

A sharp pounding noise of onrushing feet distracted the gang. It was Joan Russell galloping by the water cooler. She thundered up with a "Hi, there, everything okay?" Joan was flashing her teeth. Right together, Jackie and me: "Yes, just fine."

Joan's plain, schoolteacher face took on a serious expression. "Mike," she said, tugging at his sleeve, "you've got a get over to makeup. It's almost time for you to tape." Mike ignored her.

"So what have they had you doing?" He was speaking to me now.

"Running upstairs . . . answering phones . . . watching the wire service." I said it with a dead tone, closing my eyes a little, making a hard face. I wanted him to know by my expression that I really didn't go for the flunky role. He caught it.

"Well, this is where it all starts, the nerve center of the whole news program. This is where you learn the business." And this is where it'll all end, I was thinking, if they kept me doing this shit! My expression hadn't changed, so Mike stuck out the carrot.

"Anyway, you'll be going to the 'Eye on New York' unit day after tomorrow." I relaxed my face. That man had a way about him that I *almost* trusted.

Jackie glanced up at the big clock over the blackboard. "Oh shucks, I gotta run!" She jumped up, "See ya later!" and took off, heading for the narrow aisle, switching her cute little ass. Joan tugged Mike's sleeve again. "Mike!" she was scolding him now, "Mike, you've got to get made up!"

Mike's eyes were back searching mine. Finally her impatient voice reached him. "That's right, gotta go now." He was pulling away. "But we'll have a meeting soon with all the SEEK students and iron out any difficulties you might have." He swooped around the little bend, with Joan, then Sandra, following him. I heard the door creak open and, a few seconds later, hush closed.

The afternoon wore on in the newsroom, and as evening approached the joint began to hop.

Dudes came rushing into the newsroom like the Russians were coming; reporters, cameramen, lighting men, big bosses, little bosses, big peons, little peons, all kinds of dudes. The desk assistants, production assistants, traffic assistants all got moving, running around, back and forth like they were getting supplies and ammunition. Phones began screaming at a

65

nerve-racking tempo, typewriters opened fire at an ear-shattering rate. Dick Lobo, the Assistant Editor, and Walter Arm were shouting commands to the troops and a new name was being hollered above the din: "Dick Clark! Dick Clark!" like he was the chief medic. Turned out he was the producer. Aphrodite was sweeping in and out and the field general, News Director Lee Hanna, broke from his command post and stood with his back to the Xerox machine, his close-cropped head on fire, big blue pop-eyes glaring, watching everything, neck twisting left! right! up! down! He even tried to watch himself! And bellowing like a man gone mad! I was back and forth to the blackboard, up and down from the Film Lab, like a handball on a four-walled court. And then it was over! Silence descended.

I sagged down next to Frankie breathing hard. "Eh . . . man . . . how often . . . does this . . . happen?"

He looked up from his desk and whispered: "Every day, at the same time."

I'd just lived through the preparation of the "Six O'clock News."

My first day at CBS ended with me looking forward to the next.

The 180th Street uptown express screeched to a halt at Prospect Avenue station. I danced down the steep double stairway and raced across Westchester Avenue under the elevated steel structure, dodging between moving cars and steel pillars, yelling "Eh-AAAAAA, EhAAAAAAAAA Yaaaa!" trying to catch the number 3 bus. Just as I puffed up alongside the bus's rear exit, the goddamn driver closed the doors and pulled off, bathing me in exhaust. I stood there a few moments breathing in a nauseous mixture of curb dust and diesel fumes. It would be a half-hour or more before the next bus came along. Shit, I could walk home in less time than that. I fired up a cigarette and darted across to the west side of Prospect Avenue, quick-stepping uptown.

Both sides of the wide, treeless thoroughfare were crowded

tight with cheap clothing shops, "five-dollars-down" jewelers, "nothing-down" furniture stores, and bedbug hotels. In other stores there were printed signs in the dirt-streaked windows: "Se hable español."

I moved on, past dying childhood memories. Midway up the block the once-proud RKO Theater, where I'd spent many exciting afternoons rooting for Tarzan, Johnny Mack Brown, or Hopalong Cassidy, lay crumbled in a pile of broken timber and wounded bricks.

At the intersection of Home Street and Prospect Avenue I stopped again. The faded white building where I had once lived, and from which my Dad was thrown out, was still there.

I remembered standing in the kitchen wondering what the hell was going on as I watched my father piling all of his clothes in the middle of two old sheets spread out on the living room floor. His hands were trembling slightly, but he finally managed to tie the corners together in one big knot. With a deep, rejected sigh he pulled the bundle over his shoulder and stood there a moment staring at me like a man sentenced to die. My mother, who had been watching him silently, suddenly went into a furious rage, shouting and pointing at Dad, screaming to the two big, white policemen: "Just git him outta here. Git his ass out *now!*" One cop snatched the door open saying "C'mon fella!" like he was getting rid of an unwanted dog.

Dad's eyes grew wet as he looked at me for the last time, then he turned and shuffled slowly toward the open door. I wanted to puke when I saw the dark faces looking in from the hall. Dad hesitated at the threshold, turning back as if he'd forgotten something. Like a shot, my mother started screaming again—"OUT! OUT! OUT!"—and the two cops grabbed my father by the shoulder and shoved him backward through the door. Mom was still screaming as she rushed over to the half-open door and heaved it shut.

It made a loud BAM, like the strike of a gong signaling

the end of my childhood! Two weeks later I got my first job. I was eleven years old. I never saw or heard from my father again.

On the other side of Home Street, diagonally across from me, a bar stood between two trash-littered lots, an oasis in the desert zone. I was thirsty.

Inside, the light from a frosted-blue neon bulb drifted down over a lone cash register centered behind an L-shaped bar. Behind the short end of the L, a long-legged chicken-hipped bar maid in hot pants, with a blonde wig and a black face, was leaning over, her elbows resting on the bar, talking to a slick dude in sun shades and a dark, wide-brimmed hat. There was no one else in sight. I pulled my ass up onto a dingy, high-backed bar stool and ordered a beer.

I sucked the first one down like an open drain and called for another. When it came, I sipped on it, watching my reflection in the mirror behind the bar.

I tried to imagine how I would look if I ever got on TV. How would I sound, what style would I use—appeasing like Jensen, superior like Cronkite, or know-it-all like Keating? I wondered how much he made—fifty, sixty grand or more I bet.

I took another sip and lit up a cigarette. As the smoke escaped from my nose, the wall phone rang at the far end of the bar. I shifted my eyes following the sound and watching the slick looking dude limp over and stick the receiver to his ear. He stood with his back to me facing the wall, wide-brimmed hat cocked over one ear. There was something familiar about him. I studied him while he spoke. Then it came to me. . . . That limp! The voice! . . . Shit! . . . IT WAS ALAN BEANER!*

I hadn't seen Al since our gang-busting days about fifteen years ago. He had been president of one of the largest, baddest street gangs in New York City, and I had been his "war chief." A gang headed by a dude named "El Gato" caught a couple of our guys one night and sliced them up

* A fictitious name.

68

real bad. They didn't die, though. Al went apeshit when he heard about it and ordered El Gato killed.

A week or so later, El Gato was found in his own hallway with most of his face shot away.

I didn't wait for Al to hang up. He was something out of a dismal past. I was racing along into a sunlit future. I drained my glass, left a dollar bill on the bar, and slipped out.

5 The news staff looked on shocked! Aghast! Each person gathered in the news room seemed to be wilting in place, consciously fighting not to believe the grim scene that was being replayed on all the monitor television sets above them. Did they, the white folks, feel the same as I did? Could we both feel the same sense of impending loss?

BOBBY KENNEDY HAD BEEN SHOT!

I remember praying silently, earnestly that he would not die; for at that time I believed Senator Kennedy was one of the few white men who believed in civil rights for black people and would in time help us to accomplish that goal. I believed he was a good white man, like his late brother. Lord, please don't let him die . . . and, Lord, PLEASE don't let it be a black man that shot him.

After Senator Kennedy had been removed to the hospital, most of the news staff began drifting back dejectedly to their work areas; others drew together in small groups to discuss the crime they had just witnessed. I listened intently, as speculation as to who was behind the assassination attempt ran the gauntlet of media undesirables: the Communists, the Weathermen, the Panthers, the Klan, the Mafia, Castro?

It was about then that Freddie Cole arrived, rushing down the narrow aisle . . . late! A three-man film crew was standing, still debating, in the aisle, blocking it.

Freddie said, "excuse me please" but they didn't move so Freddie bumped into them on his way by.

"HAYYYYY, CAN'T YOU SAY EGG-SCUSE-ME, BOY?" the loud-mouthed member of the crew yelled at Freddie's back, loud enough for the whole newsroom to hear him.

That was the first overt indication of racism at CBS.

Leroy, a black assistant technician up in the film lab, had cautioned me upon our first meeting that day: "Brother, some of them white cats down in the newsroom got a new song they done made up. Call it the 'Nigger in the Newsroom,' goes to the tune of the 'Farmer in the Dell.' When you hear it, you better straighten them motherfuckers out right fast! Let 'em know you ain't takin' no SHIT!"

I hoped I would not be provoked into exploding. I knew my temper—extremely combustible! I hoped I would not hear the song.

I would be cool, had to be. My worth as a man, I felt, was inextricably attached to a career at CBS. My family was depending on me, for once proud of me, although we were broke and drowning in bills. CBS offered hope. I would hang in there! Fuck the low-class racist. I prayed I would not hear the song.

❉   ❉   ❉

The boss of the place was Lee Hanna, News Director. I couldn't imagine what he wanted when he walked over to the Traffic Desk and said, "I'd like to see you in my office in five minutes."

The door to his office was gray-blue metal, cold and imposing. I punched it three quick raps.

"Come in!" Snappy and severe.

The News Director was seated, slouched forward, behind

71

a sleek walnut-veneer desk, examining papers. Without lifting his head or easing the furrows in his brow he pointed to a chair.

"Take a seat, Jimmy, I'll be with you in a moment."

I slid into the chair and looked around at the three TV sets hung from a shelf near the ceiling, showing pictures but no sound, at the plaques and certificates on one wall, at the *Congressional Quarterlies*, almanacs, books on politics that lined another wall.

Hanna pushed back from his desk with a quick shove, folded his fists under his chin, leveled his icy blue eyes at me.

I stared back with a frozen look of my own until he broke the ice.

"What are you studying in school?" His tone was sharp and his eyes hadn't changed.

"You want me to run down my program?"

"No, that's not necessary. . . . Just what is your main interest?"

"English."

"What do you want to be?" My mind added: "When you grow up."

"A man."

"I guess you are! I mean what sort of career do you have in mind?"

"I'm not sure but I think I'd like one here, as a reporter. . . . I'm sorta nosy."

There was a long pause.

"Are you planning to train some of us as reporters?"

"We're not sure yet what any of you can do. Being a reporter is a pretty tough job!"

"I think I'm a pretty tough guy!"

"I didn't mean physically, mentally as well. Sometimes our guys get into situations where they have to make quick decisions." His eyebrows raised in phony innocence like what he was saying didn't come from his lips. He continued: "Their judgment out there can affect us back here."

72

"Give me an example."

He told me of a tense situation at a Black Power meeting when Chris Borgen and his crew had to abandon their equipment and flee through an open window because the participants at that meeting didn't care to be seen on television. I guess his point was that they valued their asses more than the story or their equipment.

"Aren't black reporters more of an asset when you've got to cover 'black news?' I mean, wouldn't they tend to do a more effective job in an area, say, like Harlem or Bed Stuy?"

"We don't assign our reporters on the basis of their race or color. We send whoever we think can do the best job!"

Did he think I believed him? After a short silence he swung from his chair and walked over to the bookshelf. He stood a moment looking up, then reached and brought down a thin black book.

"Here's something that might interest you. It might help you to understand quite a bit about television journalism."

I stood up, taking the book from his outstretched hand and peeled through a few pages.

"Of course, it doesn't contain everything. We do have to innovate. But take it with you and see what you can learn!"

A smile pinched the corners of his lips. They parted, letting the words fall out very slowly.

"I'm going to tell you something, Jimmy, that hasn't been told the other students as yet." He paused. "There are five of you here but we only intend on keeping three—the three that show the most ability. As of right now, you are all competing with one another!"

He searched my face for some sign of emotion. There was none. None that he could see. It was all raging inside my head, storming against my temples like gravel falling down a chute. His words had shocked me into a burning sense of pain and disillusion.

I looked through him, fighting back the impulse to shout: "You dirty motherfucker" and listened to my mind: One group of Whiteys had told me I'd been hired, now another

73

Whitey was saying I had to try for the job all over again, and he wasn't saying what the job would be if I got it! It was the same old shit, half-truths spread over whole lies, coming from the same people who brought the news into millions of homes every day, the same responsible people who gave the facts, told you what was happening! I wanted to get the fuck outa there!

"Is that it?" I dropped the book in the chair.

"Yes, I suppose it is." He stepped lightly across the carpet and stood gripping the door knob. "Good luck, Jimmy, stop in and see me again."

The door opened and I marched out.

The News Director's words had stunned me like an unexpected rabbit punch in the second round. I felt like quitting. Those white folks could ram CBS up their ass. But that was thinking like a fool. Maybe that's just what they wanted me to do. Why had Hanna said he'd told only me and not the rest of the students? Because he liked me or something? Could it be that he wanted *me* to tell them, or did he plan to call them in, one at a time, and tell each one about the three coins in his pocket then wait to see which of the five could turn the most tricks? Did Mike know about this shit too? What the fuck was really going on? I decided to stow away my questions and feelings. I'd bring them back at the right time, when Mike held his Friday luncheon. I walked back to the Traffic Desk full of suppressed anger.

❁   ❁   ❁

A sharp Bing! Bing! Bing! pierced the air. I froze! Bing! Bing! Bing! Oh, shit! A bulletin from the wire service! I sprinted into the Wire Room, sprang for the nearest machine, ripped the sheet from its mouth, pivoted, bulled past two late-arriving white desk assistants, and got the message over to Walter Arm. He praised me like a pet dog, then told me to get back and wait for any follow-up.

74

The two white dudes were inside mopping up when I returned to the Wire Room, slowly tearing teletyped copies of the story from the other machines. They looked at me with envious eyes, pissed off that I'd been first to the action. I leaned against the locker, arms folded across my chest, watching them, a smug smile on my face. I'd made points with the bossman and showed up them smart-ass white dudes at the same time. Nigger in the newsroom, huh!

After they left, I got busy collecting the old sheets of news, rolling them up, and stuffing them onto shelves above the machines.

Freddie Cole came into the room silently and stood looking at the copy on one of the teletypes.

"Eh, Jimmy."

"Yeah, what's happening?"

"Look man, I got something to tell you." His face was flushed.

"Hey man, you gotta problem?"

"Maaann, I just heard some shit that I swear I didn't like." Tears began from under his glasses.

"Eh, man. WHAT'S WRONG?"

'Shit, you don't know, but that rednecked, long-nosed motherfucker upstairs made me so mad I could'a killed him! So help me God, if it wasn't for this job I'd a—"

"HEY MAN," I hollered at him, "TELL ME WHAT THE FUCK HAPPENED, WILL YUH!"

"You heard about the new song, ain't cha? The 'Nigger in the Newsroom' song?"

"Yeah, I heard of it."

"Well, that sonofabitch upstairs must've thought that I was white or something, because he sang it around me up in the darkroom, then he started telling me some bullshit about the colored 'gals' he was fucking, telling me what he did to them and how crazy they were for his big white dick."

So what, I thought, white dudes probably all talk like that about black pussy.

75

"Then he started in on you, man." My whole body tightened. "He said that you looked like an orangutan. Said your momma and daddy had to be apes!"

"THAT WEASELY MOTHERFUCKER SAID THAT SHIT 'BOUT ME?" I bellowed it like a wounded animal. I bolted for the door. Freddie grabbed my arm.

"Hold on man, why don't you wait and tell Mr. Keating!"

"What the fuck you sayin'? He ain't said nothing 'bout Keating or his momma and daddy. HE WAS TALK'N 'BOUT ME AND MINE!" I tore my arm away from Freddie and burst through the open door, racing for the dim-lit stairwell leading to the film lab.

I shoved open the door leading into the second-floor corridor. WHAM! It slammed against the wall, and I stamped into the corridor, breathing like a bull. Leroy was alone in the film lab.

"Hey man, where's that long-nosed motherfucker?"

"Ronnie?"

"THE WHITE DUDE, MAN!" Who the fuck he think I meant?

"Yeah, Ronnie. . . . He took a break."

"Well, when he gets back sound him that I want to see his ass!" Leroy knew his boss was in trouble.

On my way back downstairs, I decided it was a good thing that moleface bastard wasn't there. With my record for assaulting white folks, my ass would be on its way to the slammers by now. Still, I had to figure out how I was gonna fix his ass. I'd been weight-lifting about two years and weighed 190 pounds on a five-foot-five frame. If he thought I looked like an ape, I'd act like one—go ape shit an' clean it up with him!

A half-hour later, he came strolling around the bend. He must've just finished eating because there was a pleased look on his face.

I was thinking about what I was going to do—how I'd stomp and bust up his ass before the other Whiteys came to the rescue. One catch, though—I had to make the punk-

76

ass faggot call me something or swing at me. I'd learned that from my last run-in with a Whitey—a sonofabitch that I worked for who put his foot in my ass. I went to jail for attempted murder; there were no witnesses for me that time. This time I wasn't gonna give them jive police the chance to lock my butt up. It was gonna be self-defense all the way. With witnesses!

He'd been upstairs fifteen minutes—plenty of time for Leroy to tell him I was hunting. I took my time climbing the stairs, building up rage, drawing strength.

Leroy's head popped out the door when I was halfway down the hall.

"Hey, yo boss back yet?" I hollered. As he nodded yes, Moleface stepped into the hallway.

"You wanted to see me?"

"You motherfuckin' right, shithead." I was in his face now, running down what Freddie had told me, talking loud, drawing a crowd. My witnesses! I was up against his chest now, roaring what I'd do to him if I heard it again. The white bitches had come out into the hallway, the ones Moleface flirted with. I really punked him when I noticed them.

"Now you say you sorry, BOY!" I had his ass going now.

"Say, Mr. Watson, SIR, please take mercy on my stupid ass and leave it in one piece—SAY IT!"

He vibrated from rage, or shame or fear or maybe all three, but the molefaced motherfucker said it.

I'd proved my superiority to a white man in the best way —fear! Ain't that how he does it? I had degraded him in front of his white women! God damn! That was the best part!

* * *

Keating casually brought up the incident at lunch on Friday.

"What happened over in the newsroom the other day, Jimmy?"

"What do you mean Mr. Keating?" I stuck a forkful of

77

lemon pie into my mouth. Who was he kidding with? Everyone on the news staff knew what had happened.

"I understand that you were almost involved in a fight with someone from the film lab."

"Wouldn'a been no fight." That brought on a snicker from the apprentices seated around the table.

"No?"

"No, I'd-a just busted his ass!" Everyone burst out laughing except Mike and Sandra.

"Look, Jimmy, use your head. Don't you know if you had assaulted the man you would have been fired and possibly arrested? You should have come to me with the problem."

"COME TO YOU?" I stared at him hard! "Looka here, man, was you mad at the motherfucker? Was you gonna kick his ass? What'd I need you for?"

Keating's tone became sharp:

"I would have been able to put him on the carpet . . . brought it to the attention of his superiors. He could have been warned that it just might cost him his job if he shot off his mouth like that again! We know you've got muscles, but what would beating him up have gained you? What you were about to do was certainly not rational."

Rational! The word bit into me. I put my fork down and glared at him. The sonofabitch, hell, no, he would never think it was rational for a black man to speak about putting his foot in a white man's ass. No, that was insane. Everyone was waiting for my response. Sandra alone looked down her nose at me, sure that I had none.

"Mr. Keating," I began slowly, "I don't tell myself to be rational when someone calls me and my parents apes. I gets my nose open! Was that dude Ronnie acting rational when he said that shit? How you gonna be rational with somebody who ain't? Suppose it had happened to you? Would you have went running to tell some other man to do something about it when you supposed to be a man yourself? And if you did go tell some other dude, wouldn't he be thinking that he's a bigger man than you—maybe like your daddy?

"I'll come to you in a minute 'bout a job problem, but this was personal. I wipes my own ass and flushes my own shit. You see, my way is like preventive medicine. That cracker knows now if he don't act rational with me, I ain't gonna act rational with him, and that goes for the rest of the crackers around here!"

"It's true that Ronnie acted like an ass. But he wouldn't have gotten into trouble if you had assaulted him. You would! You can't just run around beating up everyone who says something you don't like."

"Maybe I can't, but I ain't gonna come crying to you. Did Ronnie come crying to you? Did you tell him that he just can't run around calling people's moms and pops apes? I DID!"

Mike and I looked at each other, knowing that I was drawing boundaries: You, Mr. Keating, will never be able to dictate or predict my reactions to anything. You might be in charge here, but you ain't in control of me. If you thought, during that interview, I was some kind'a faggot nigger with muscles, you were so wrong. I want the job, not the bullshit.

I stared into his marble blue eyes as I thought that. His face had drawn tight and he was losing color. He was not used to being overpowered in any way, mentally or physically, but I had him retreating. His face was slowly relaxing and I could feel him thinking: All right, nigger, you looked pretty good this time. But this is my program and you ain't gonna fuck it up; there'll be a way to handle you; you'll either shape up or ship out, goddammit!

Well, he was full of shit. The goddamn program wasn't gonna work because of him, but because of us—the black people in it.

*　*　*

Jimmy Watson had caught my attention in the first interview of the apprenticeship candidates in the spring, and

79

my interest never dimmed throughout the first summer of the program.

Like most short men, he had an aggressiveness about his body, thrusting it before his audience to make it larger than life. The muscles he had developed in his arms, legs, and torso gave him a rolling gait and a stiffness of movement that drew attention, like an armored car moving down Fifth Avenue among the taxis and buses.

And if you had not noticed his body and the broad, inquisitive face sitting atop it, you could not miss his voice. It was heavy and rich with blood, unmistakably black and male—a powerful, resonant voice, perfect for broadcasting, I thought. He had a theatrical ability of changing its style—from black street hip, through college-man insouciance, to white middle-class politesse. Like his clothes—gymnasium weightlifter slick, through undergraduate sweatshirt and jeans, to Madison Avenue suit and tie, complete with slim metal attaché case and a cheery good morning.

He was older than the others, married, with kids; had served in the Marines; had been convicted of assault; spoke intelligently; and was said by a teacher at City College to be a promising writer. He seemed ambitious, and he intrigued me.

But he worried me. I sensed a violence in him, and a temper, and a tense effort to keep it all under control—a rage within.

When I heard about the incident in the Film Lab, I wanted to move vigorously and quickly to save him from himself, to let him know that CBS was no place for him to let slip his self-control. He had an assault conviction on his record and under normal circumstances probably would not have been hired by CBS because of it. But this was a special program and, as I had pointed out to the Personnel Department, we were not going to find many vigorous young men from the ghetto without a record. A fistfight on the job would do him in, however, and cause other repercussions, not the least of which would be to heighten newsroom hostility.

And besides, he looked like prime material to become a television newsman: appearance, voice, intelligence, confident manner, and those mouths to feed at home. I wanted graduates from my program, not black folk heroes.

I confronted him on the issue, telling him he should let me handle the discipline of others, not rely on his fists. He was polite enough in his rebuff of my recommendation, but at the same time he gave me his message directly and clearly. He treasured his dignity and self-sufficiency and he would permit nothing, including promises of golden careers at CBS, to diminish that sense of himself.

I backed off from a direct conflict with him, letting him know that as I taught him he could teach me.

I liked the authenticity and directness of the man and wanted to know more of the strength he used to keep himself intact in such a hostile society.

Later that summer he came into my office and handed me a book.

"This explains me."

It was by two black psychiatrists, and its title was *Black Rage*.

6 Bob was the boss of the show, producer of "Eye on New York," Channel Two's weekly documentary, a young Jew dude who looked a lot like Danny Thomas.

"Jimmy, you're here to work *with* us, not for black decoration! I want you to take an active part in whatever we do. Don't hold back—give us your opinion!"

Bob had a big nose. It took up most of his face, and as he spoke his nose contracted and expanded like a flexing biceps.

"I know you can make a strong contribution to us because of your different background, your different experiences, lifestyle."

He was seated stiffly behind the desk in his office, and I was on a folding chair listening to his introductory speech for my new assignment in the News Department. My eyes darted around while he spoke. The office was small—a lot of papers, some books, a desk, the two chairs we were sitting in. That's all. The producer of a television show and he didn't have an office big enough to fuck in!

"You bring a different viewpoint with you, another dimension, you might say."

In between rapid-fire sentences, he masturbated his mouth

with a long green cigar, swirling it with his tongue, drawing it in and out with his lips.

I had met him downstairs in the Projection Room with
the other members of the "Eye on New York" crew—Steve,
the film editor; Joe, the cameraman; and Louie, the lighting
technician. Louie was the dude who had shouted the "Hey,
boy" routine at Freddie Cole in the newsroom the previous
day, and he looked hard at me when he shook my hand. I
squeezed his and gave him a wink.

"I've had the experience before," Bob said, "with black
guys I've worked with being used as props, you know what
I mean?"

I nodded. Damn right I knew what he meant! He waited
for me to say something, drumming his heavy fingers on the
desk. I looked into his small, dark eyes. Was he trying to
con me? What made him think I came here expecting to
play the fuck'n butler? There was something sly about this
dude. I decided to roll with his con by telling the truth.

"Well, I'm glad you feel that way, Bob. I've been waiting
for just such an opportunity."

He snatched the long, green cigar from his mouth and
continued speaking in his high-pitched voice:

"If you do well here with us, I'll try and keep you."

I guess he thought that made me feel good. Talk was free
and folks gave away promises. He relit his cigar, and in a
blue-gray cloud excused himself: "I have to finish writing a
script. Stay with Steve the rest of the day and you'll go out
with the film crew tomorrow. How's that?"

I said it was okay, but I didn't mean it. I wanted to get
out on the streets, see what's going on, not stay cooped up
in that factory downstairs. But if I had to wait one more day,
I'd wait one more day. He smiled. I smiled. Then he shoved
his hand and I wrapped mine around it. We looked like a
Labor Party emblem.

"I hope you'll enjoy working with us, Jimmy. See ya
later."

Maybe the dude was all right, except that he sounded like he almost felt sorry for me, like he knew my being there was only a game, a game he didn't want to play but was already in. And I kind of felt sorry for him—a big-time producer with a pup tent for an office. Shit, how much cash could he be making?

*　*　*

Bob led the crew over to the Museum of Natural History to film a story on a woman who had gunned down a polar bear and given it to the museum as a present. I stood a few feet away listening to Bob chatting with the broad while Joe and Louie set up their equipment. I gazed at the embalmed animals sealed in glass cages around the massive room. The cages had artificial turf, painted mountains and valleys, and fake trees to remind the animals of the life they once knew —even a waterfall that wasn't wet.

I took a good look at the polar bear, the arctic scene surrounding him, then stared at his slayer. The bitch looked rich, dressed down in a big-game outfit, boots, a wide safari hat on her gray head, and large, expensive stones sparkling on her fingers. Bob was kissing her ass, and their voices echoed through the balconies and into my ears. They were talking about money, things that money bought—safaris, planes, yachts, estates. Bob noticed me watching, stopped licking butt for a moment, and called me over to meet the rich-ass ho'. She looked at him like he was out of his mind. Shit, she didn't want to meet no NIGGER! But Bob wanted her to know that he had one, a tame one! I stuck out my hand, the old ho' made a flimsy effort to raise hers but it hung bent at the wrist as though the stones on her boney fingers would let the hand go no higher. Fuck it! I grabbed her hand and squeezed it, then let it drop. The hand felt old and cold and looked it, the veins like blue worms under cracked skin. I smiled and her eyes glowed with hatred.

I laughed inside as I walked back to the murdered bear's

cage. He seemed to be grinning. When the crew was ready, the huntress took her place next to the glassed-in bear with her rifle under her arm. She stared at me, her face twitching nervously, and patted her big gun. She wanted to shoot me. I wanted to feel her ass.

That kind of shit wasn't getting to me, though. I was digging the role of the brick-hard, bold-ass nigger. Having fun, but not making no money. Seventy-five bucks a week. But that was only temporary, so I thought. I hadn't been on the job long enough. I'd get mine after I'd learned something, like being a producer.

Bob had been telling me lately that he was surprised to see how quickly I was catching on to the job and how pleased he was with the suggestions I had been making, especially those I had given him on interviewing people. It was his recognition of my ability, his continuing praise and encouragment, that helped me to decide I wanted to be a producer. I began to feel I was a part of the "Eye on New York" crew.

The work was interesting, exciting, and varied, with a greater creative range than straight-up reporting; you chose your subject, developing it into a story as you went along. As a producer, I would be noticed, I'd be a professional, I'd be a success. It was a job I knew I could do.

The "Eye on New York" unit gave me a chance also to watch big Jim Jensen in action. Besides being the station's resident news star—the anchorman of the news broadcasts —he also narrated many of the "Eye" documentaries. I didn't like his "I'm-great-so-kiss-my-ass" attitude. He interviewed some people like they were shit, imbeciles, idiots, morons, jokes!

"What has this doctor being here meant to the neighborhood?" Jensen was asking an old, ragged Puerto Rican obviously drunk. "Would you like to see more doctors like him come in here? . . . When was the last time you were examined by a doctor?"

The guy hadn't answered any of Jensen's questions, but Jim kept on. The old Spic looked down at the mike, rub-bing his dirty beard, but didn't answer. Big Jim smiled and tried again.

"How far would you have to travel to get treatment if the doctor wasn't here? Where would you go?"

The old Spic picked at his belly through a rip in his greasy T-shirt and blinked dumbly.

We were filming a story about a doctor on East 10th Street who was said to be treating the niggers and Spics in the area and not making money. Shit! No doctor does something for nothing; maybe he was experimenting on people or trying to hustle a grant, but nobody do something for nothing!

Bob was bustling through the excited crowd, picking out faces for Jim to interview in front of the camera. I was helping Joe the cameraman, and Louie was leaning against a building nearby eating an ice cream pop.

Everybody wanted to get on TV, so everybody was pushing and shoving, trying to get close to Jensen. He was eating it up, acting sassy in his high-powered clothes.

A huge Puerto Rican wearing a black beret broke through the crowd like King Kong and stood next to the old Spic. From the fierce look that big motherfucker was giving Jensen I figured some shit was about to start. Jensen grinned at the mean-looking dude. The dude didn't crack a smile, just kept clenching and unclenching his black-gloved hands.

Jensen smiled at the crowd and repeated his question to the old wino: "Where would you go for treatment if the doctor wasn't here?"

Suddenly the wino craned his face up to Jensen, forgetting about the microphone, and slobbered: "All the way to Bellevue."

Jensen flinched from the old dude's foul breath, said "thank you," then glared at Bob to warn him that the next one better not be crazy. And that's when the big black beret made his move. He stepped up to Jensen, stared him up and down like he'd fuck him in the ass, and snarled:

"Pack up your shit and get the fuck offa 10th Street now!"

The dude spoke like he was talking to a used-up whore!

86

Jensen wasn't gonna take that shit, not him, not big-time motherfucker Jim Jensen!!! All he did was stand there with his mouth half open, looking like somebody hit him with a bucket of shit! Like a punk.

The dude turned around and stomped back through the crowd like he'd scalped everybody's balls. Which he had.

Joe, struck dumb, had his camera pointed to the sky like a sawed-off bazooka and his hand locked on Bob's elbow, sweating his ass off. Bob chewed nervously on his cigar as if he wanted to leave. That's all, just leave!

I strained to keep in the laughter. I ain't never seen Whiteys so scared.

Louie waited until the black beret was out of sight before he rushed over to Jensen. "Who the fuck does he think he is?" He said it nasty, gargled in his throat before he threw it out.

I was ready to leave. Jensen wasn't. "I'm gonna see about this!" He made a break through the crowd. Bob stopped him.

"I wouldn't fool around with those guys. They're MILITANTS!"

Jim flared. "Well, what the fuck are we gonna do, pack up and run because some punk told us to get out?"

Yeah man, I was thinking, that's a good idea; makes a whole lot of sense! I used to hang out in the neighborhood and I knew where them dudes were coming from. The number of black berets was increasing among the crowd.

Bob wanted to save face. "No, call the cops!"

Call the cops! You SISSY—the word ran through my mind —you goddamn sissy! I didn't like cops. They shoot black folks in a minute. Saw one shoot a kid over in the 70s. The kid was black; the cop was white. Big Jim didn't want no cops either. He wasn't that big a punk.

"Fuck that. I'm gonna find out what the hell's going on! C'MON, JIMMY!"

Now wasn't that a bitch! What made the cute ass think I was his fucking bulldog?

87

Jensen took off through the crowd sure that I was right behind him. I hadn't moved. Bob looked at me. Joe looked at me. Louie looked at me. They were thinking that Jensen might get murdered if I didn't go along with him. After all, I was one of the natives. The tribe might not get into a frenzy if I was there. Save the sahib!

Shit, they were crazy. Ain't nothing a nigger hates more than a nigger helping a Whitey against another nigger. I could get wasted just for being with Jensen! But then . . . on the other hand . . . maybe going with him might help me use him later. I wanted to be a producer and I knew how things worked at CBS. You had to be clicked up to get the job you wanted. Helping Jensen might do that. But I wasn't down for no fights, and I wasn't going to risk my ass in one.

Jim was midway up the block waiting for me, staring at some dudes around the entrance to an old public building across the street. The dudes were dressed in black berets and army field jackets. Hatred hardened their faces as we crossed the street and approached them. Jensen asked for their leader. They looked at me like I was a traitor.

"Mr. Carson is up on the fourth floor," one of them said.

I knew what they were thinking: white man's nigger!

Big Jim held his head high, rushing up the stairs two at a time, passing Puerto Ricans coming down. They eyed him like he was the devil. I lagged behind. It was his show, I was going along as a spectator. Jensen waited for me when he reached the fourth floor, looking down a hallway that was packed with dudes wearing black berets and field jackets, tough-looking niggers and Spics, scowling. Jim slowed his pace and cooled his cocky walk as we passed through and I heard them mutter "honkies." So me, too, huh? Now I was a goddamn honky!

A dark-haired Spanish broad was sitting at a table in the hall knitting.

"Where is Mr. Carson?" Big Jim's tone was tough.

She placed her knitting on the table, then calmly said

that Mr. Carson was busy in his office, her eyes indicated a door across the hall.

Big Jim said he wanted to see Mr. Carson now and would she tell him Mr. Jensen was here.

The broad picked up her knitting, sucked her teeth, and said Jim would have to wait; she could not interrupt Mr. Carson.

Jim made a face, looked down at me, didn't say nothing, then began pacing back and forth in front of the tables. The hallway grew dark with black berets as more dudes kept coming in. I eased back, increasing the distance between me and Jensen as the dudes began to crowd loosely around us. Jensen noticed my move and kept edging closer, pretending he had something to say to me. I stepped back a little farther. I didn't want to hear nothing!

Then Sonny Carson burst from his office talking heavy shit. "What do you want, HONKY?"

Jensen's big jaws tightened. "The name is Jim Jensen and I want to know who's ordering me and my news crew to leave the block?"

Carson gnashed his teeth, flashed a demon's eye at me, and snarled: "I am, honky!"

"For what reason and by whose authority?"

"By my own fuck'n authority, honky! I don't want them fuck'n cameras on the goddamn block an' they better not be there tomorrow! Do you understan', mannnnnnn? Only time we see you honkies down here is when you hustlin' MY PEOPLE!" Carson's Afro seemed electrified as he tore the words from his mouth and beat them in Big Jim's face.

"WE go where the news is and we don't hustle people, or whatever you call it," Jim shot back.

Carson roared like a madman and flung out his arms like he was ready to be nailed to a cross. "The fuck'n cameras excite the people. You got them running in the streets. Somebody could get hurt—maybe some of you honkies!"

The dudes in the crowd had their eyes fixed on me as he spoke. I think they wanted to beat me to death.

89

"We can't help it if people follow us. We're only out doing a job and if the job happens to be on 10th Street we go to 10th Street!"

I liked the way Jensen was talking back. He damn sure wasn't punking out. But his mouth might get *us* in a rumble.

"They better not be there tomorrow, honky, I'm telling you!" Carson's voice rose louder as he leered at Big Jim. Jim looked over to me like I was supposed to sic 'em! I stepped back slightly, looking innocent. I wasn't his fucking bodyguard, and I wanted to let them mean-looking dudes know it! Their expressions didn't change. I was the white man's nigger. I could see it in their faces.

Then Big Jim stunned Carson. "You can't just tell the press we can't come on this block. Who the hell do you think you are anyway?"

The black berets tensed up, getting ready to jump us, only waiting for Carson's signal. I got ready to fight!

Carson clenched his teeth and hissed the words slow and easy. "If you honkies come in here tomorrow there's gonna be trouble. Believe me, yuh gonna get fucked up, so help me God!"

Big Jim glanced at me again. He was making me mad. These dudes already had me down as an Uncle Tom; what the fuck was Jensen trying to do?

Carson closed the meeting by simply moving out among his cohorts, issuing orders for things to be done in the community—collecting clothes, food, acting like we weren't there.

Big Jim stood watching like he had more to say. Enough was enough, I started back down the hall. Carson might change his mind and start kicking asses in the next minute. Big Jim pulled himself together and followed behind me, his superior attitude returning the closer we came to the exit.

I felt shitty. Why had those dudes assumed I was Jensen's flunky, and why had Jensen thought so too?

We were almost to the car when Jensen turned to me.

"Jimmy, do you know what's wrong with those guys? What do they want?"

"Do you?" What the fuck was he asking me for? I wasn't no goddamn prophet. Ask the Gallup Poll, motherfucker!

Jim didn't answer my question. His mind was on the crowd, which was moving in mass behind us and circling the car. Someone shouted: "Get these honkies offa 10th Street!"

As I reached the door and dove inside, something hard hit the roof. Oh shit, I thought, I might get lynched by my own people! Jensen shoved in quickly behind me. I looked past Joe through the window—niggers and Spics all around us. My stomach knotted.

"GET THESE HONKIES OFFA 10TH STREET!" They were all shouting now.

"Let's get the fuck outta here," Jensen yelled, "these fucking bastards are crazy!"

Louie floored the accelerator.

✿ ✿ ✿

Mike was still holding his Friday afternoon meetings, which were becoming more of a farce each week. He'd ask how it was going and did any of us have anything to say. Our only response was that we were "fine."

With the possible exception of Sandra, we were all suspicious of him. We knew each of our supervisors sent him a confidential report on us, and we knew, too, that we were supposed to be competitors. Competition, we suspected, was nothing more than CBS's attempt to keep us docile, a disguised effort to get us to "Tom."

It was at the end of one of those brief meetings that Mike asked me to stay after everyone had gone. I sank back down in my seat. So this is it, huh? I been half-ass expecting it. This is the payoff for telling him off about the Ronnie thing. This is where I get my walking papers.

"Jimmy, how would you like to go on the air?" WHAT? It took a moment to believe he was serious.

"What would I be doing?" It really didn't matter, but I had to say something to keep from babbling YesYesYesYes-YesYesYes!

"An appearance on 'Opportunity Line' with Jim Jensen and Joan Murray. You'd tell something about your being a SEEK student and working in the program here at CBS. What you think of it, etc. Whatdya say, like to give it a try?"

"I'll give it a try." Oh, God, wait till I get home with this. I'm really gonna be on TV! "Opportunity Line." That's the station's new show I seen that tells people who ain't got no job where they can find one. Man, everybody's gonna see me. I'm gonna be on television. Right On!

For the first time since I'd known him, Keating seemed to be aware that he'd reached me, deeply. He was staring at me now, the wisp of a smile on his lips and the slightest twinkle in his eyes. I felt relaxed under his gaze, and he knew from the warmness of my smile that I knew he had arranged everything, and that I was grateful.

✿ ✿ ✿

Bob was on his feet clapping five seconds before Adam switched on the lights.

"Great stuff! Great, I tell yuh! It's GREAT!"

"Whatdya think of it, Adam?" Adam Clayton Powell III adjusted his glasses.

"I think it's good, Bob, especially that last line where she calls him a Communist. That's a good scene."

Bob grinned, then called across the room to Steve, who was rewinding the film. "Whadya think Steve? How'd ya like it?"

"Ah, ah . . . er, well . . . uh, hmm, to be truthful with you, Bob, it's all right, except that we have only two good interviews on film. The old lady at the end that Adam likes and the minister in the beginning. The rest is empty. The people don't take sides. If we had two or three more making strong statements pro or con then we'd have it."

"You're absolutely right, Steve. I was thinking the same thing myself. Adam, you'll have to take the crew back out to Jersey this afternoon. Shoot as many feet as you have to and make sure and get people on both sides who feel strongly about the minister. Go to the shopping mall, that'd be a good place to set up. Jimmy knows where it is— What's the matter?" Adam was shaking his head.

"I can't go this afternoon, Bob. I'm working on a project with Earl Ubell the next few days."

"Oh, shit!" Bob ripped the cigar from his mouth. "Dammit, it's Wednesday already and Hanna will want to see it Friday afternoon." Bob took a deep breath and shoved the cigar back in his jaws, cocking his head, looking at me.

"Jimmy!" His chewed, unlit cigar shot toward my face. "You've been out there with me from the beginning. Think you can handle the interviews and get what we need?"

"Of course!"

"All right. You leave at one o'clock. You'll be the producer."

YEAH, MAN!

There were dark clouds far to the east forming above the New York City skyline as we reached the crest of a steep grade. Below, the New Jersey Turnpike weaved through patches of burnt meadows, then gradually veered off to the southwest. We drove on down, passing the scorched Secaucus pig lands at maximum speed. Two more exits to go, and I'd get the chance to do my thing.

I looked at Joe nodding next to me, drugged by too much manicotti, meatballs, and linguine. We shoulda dropped his fat ass off in Secaucus, Adam too, if he'd been along. I was glad as hell he wasn't. I mighta got a shot before this except for Adam always being there. He didn't do nothing on the show that I couldn't do, but he did have a congressman for a daddy. Maybe I was getting this shot to see if I could do the job as Bob's assistant. Maybe my appearance on "Opportunity Line" had been a test. Shit, I'd done my number real cool for the cameras, handled Jensen's questions like a pro, and bathed co-host Joan Murray with charm. Man, everybody who'd seen it, including the Inner Crowd, said I had looked real good! Not long after that, Jackie and me began appearing on a weekly TV show with some other SEEK students. This must be the next step. Bob said I would be the producer today on a documentary about a controversial white minister active in the civil rights crusade. Dig that shit! Jimmy Watson, Associate Producer of "Eye on New York"—NO!—the Producer of "Eye on New York"! Kiss my ass! How 'bout that? So why was Harry Arouh, one of the WCBS-TV News correspondents, riding up front, yapping with Louie? Bob had said I would do the interviewing!

The exit came up and Joe woke up sweating as we went past the toll booth and drove up the ramp to the highway. A few minutes west of the turnpike the rustic-painted buildings of the shopping mall sprawled to the right like a twentieth-century trading post set down along the green-edged tract of red brick ranch homes. Louie swung smoothly into the parking lot, cruising slowly past the food markets, clothing shop, and drive-in bank. When he found a space near Woolworth's he parked, and I climbed out, followed by Arouh.

"This spot is fine, Jimmy. I can stand here by the entrance and catch the people for interviews as they come out."

He could catch the people! I held my breath, gritting my teeth.

"Oh, and Jimmy, look, if we're going to get these people to express themselves truthfully on film it's best that you stand somewhere off to one side. We wouldn't want them to think you're with us."

My insides collapsed!

I went down to the far side of the mall, lit up a Salem, and whistled smoke at the fifty-thousand-dollar homes. What the fuck was I—an antitruth serum? My black face was gonna keep them pure-ass white folks from speaking the truth? What the fuck was I doing here playing Whitey's game. Me, the PRODUCER! Ain't that some shit! A jive-ass con game!

94

Bob and his c'mon-black-boy-and-I'll-give-you-a-shot; we gonna get down together. Me the producer! Dirty white bastards! Stupid me to go for that shit. Well, Arouh had just stomped some sense into my head, laid the black tax on me! Whitey always made you pay for your blackness with pain! Not only Arouh, but all those two-legged white dogs pissin' in your face and snappin' at your spirit. Shaking your hand, pulling you in while they got a foot stuck in your stomach keeping you out. Push 'n' pull, pumping shit on yo' dreams.

I didn't belong here! I can't be nothing here but a fuck'n flunky, I see that now. If I'm ever gonna get what I want outa life, if I'm really gonna make it, I got to do it with my own people. I got to get something and hustle. Whitey ain't givin' up nothing. Face it, ain' never gonna be no producer—or no reporter either—that's for Whiteys.

I'm gonna be something, though, gonna git me some cash, goddammit! You don't need no title when you got cash. When you got that, you got it all! Lookit my man Stan— he got plenty cash and he don't work for nobody. Said he was gonna stop over the house and talk to me about something. Hope he makes it soon. If he drops me some coke to hustle with I'll show these motherfuck'n Whiteys how much I need them. Reporter! Pro-duce-ser! Shit! Oh, I'll keep this white man's nigger job cause I want to stay on TV; keeps me looking good to the family and the folks around the block. But I'm gonna get me something to make me some cash. Ain't gonna depend on no white man job for no future. Gonna go out here and grab me one!

By the time we got back to New York I had but one ambition: to be a money-making cocaine hustler.

   ❄   ❄   ❄

I was on my way to Studio 46 in Broadcast Center for the daily editorial taping when Jimmy stopped me in the corridor.

"I'd like to talk to you, Mike."

"Shoot." I was in a rush.

"No, I'd like to sit down and talk. When can I stop by your office?"

"Come over tomorrow afternoon, around 3. I have some time then."

His face was serious and dark when he entered my office the next day and pulled a chair close to my desk. He told me what had happened in the supermarket parking lot with Harry Arouh. I caught the distress in his voice and eyes. I didn't know what to say to him—the event at the supermarket had undermined a lot of words I and others had uttered.

I was not surprised by what had happened. Newsmen are not noted for their sensitivity. But I told Jimmy I was surprised, that I would try to correct the situation in some way, and that he should hang on. He seemed to be satisfied with my answer.

Some action seemed to be called for on my part: If whites could interview blacks, blacks could interview whites. But I could not figure out what action I should take. I had no authority over Arouh. I was the Editorial Director, he worked for the News Director, Lee Hanna. If I complained to Hanna, chances were he would regard Watson as a trouble-maker and the possibility of Jimmy's joining that department would be diminished. If I brought the matter to the General Manager it would increase the friction developing between the News Department and me over my editorials sympathizing with the black cause in the school decentralization struggle that was heading rapidly toward an abrasive and divisive citywide school strike. And based on previous conversations with executives in the News Department, I expected that their reaction to the incident would be to conclude that Watson was overly sensitive, a crybaby, not tough enough to be a newsman. Whatever turn I considered looked to be negative, either for Watson, or for the apprentice-ship program—or both.

In any case, Jimmy Watson was scheduled for rotation next week and he would be working directly for me, researching and writing editorials in an office adjoining mine in Black Rock. So I let the matter slide, feeling vaguely guilty for doing so.

I was looking forward to his coming. I wanted to see first-hand whether he could write. And I was impressed with his reaction to the Arouh incident. He hadn't meekly accepted it as part of the dues to be paid. He had made an issue of it. I admired that. I wanted to get to know him better.

7 The dark blue pants fell crumpled over a polished pair of cordovans, and the stall beside me erupted in a violent fart accompanied by the sound of loose shit striking water. I shut off my nostrils and quickly folded my silver-foil as the stench seeped under the partition. I didn't like sniffing coke in the men's room, but it was the safest place I knew of at Black Rock.

Ugh, damn! I wished that sonofabitch would send that stuff on its way!

I didn't go for my assignment at Black Rock either, but it was the next apprenticeship rotation. Black Rock was headquarters for all the CBS big honcho's, including Keating. I was right in the motherfucker's lap, and, man, he was bugging the hell outta me asking about that editorial he didn't know I hadn't started writing yet. My mind wasn't on no fuck'n editorial. I was hustlin' now and needed a new connection. Reno, a small time coke supplier who had given me my start, had been busted last week. Dealing cocaine sure was big fun; saw more money in a week than I saw in a month from CBS. And the bitches—goddamn—they sure git up off the pussy easy when you put some coke up their noses. I'd damn sure be ready for them too! The fuck'n stuff made me feel like my whole body was a living, pulsating dick, craving to be in a woman, sheathed in one!

Another loud fart split the air and again the splash and putrid odor. Good God, what did this buzzard eat to make him smell so bad! I cleared my throat noisily and flushed the toilet, hoping the stinking motherfucker would take the hint. Damn, I wanted another sniff of blow before I went back to getting through the day, but I wasn't about to open my silverfoil package of cocaine until the air cleared. Cocaine absorbed odors. Damn my fuck'n luck! Why did Reno have to get busted now. Ava was really on my ass about moving since the junkies broke in the house—dirty motherfuckers stole the TV and the silverware Alma gave us for a wedding present, now she was raisin' hell. Ava was right. The neighborhood we lived in was no place to bring up kids.

Shit, I'd-a had enough money to move to Long Island in a few more months. Damn, just when I was starting to get clean too; wearing tailor-made suits, looking just as sharp as these paddies at Black Rock. This bad hookup I got on now cost $225. Well that's how it is when you're dealing for a small-time dude. I had to find another connection, and soon. If only I could get a play with Stan. Man, he's big time.

Man, what's this dude gonna do, shit all day? I wish the hell he'd hurry up! Keating should be in by now, and he might be asking where I'm at. Ain't no sense getting fired when I'm a TV star, ha ha. There's something about that dude; ever since he put me on television he's been acting different. Last night was the second time we been out drinking since I been over here at Black Rock, and each time it was him inviting me—wonder why. It's got to be something more than keeping my morale up. Ha, my morale. Shit, this jive-ass job is a motherfucking front! If it wasn't for my appearances on the weekly TV show, I wouldn't even be here.

Whew! And I can't stay in here much longer; gotta have one more blow. Hurry up, goddamit! I flushed and coughed again. The dude responded with a blast that roared through the shithouse. You rotten sonofabitch. What the fuck was

99

he trying to do? Why didn't he do that at home instead of drenching this place in shit vapor. I wrapped the foil back in my handkerchief, left the stall, stuffed the handkerchief in my inside jacket pocket, and, after checking my nose, hair, and double-breasted suit in the mirror, opened the door and swaggered out into the twenty-fifth floor lobby. I'd just had enough cocaine: feeling good and HORNY!

"Good morning, Jimmy. Like that suit!" The receptionist, a raven-haired Latin with a flashy smile, put down her magazine. She was real friendly.

"Thank you, Lola, when you going in *Playboy*?" I gave her an appraising stare as I swept through the reception area. It was easy to imagine her golden nakedness, the stem of a red rose trapped between her teeth, and a white, silk-sheeted bed.

The door was open when I passed Mike's office. He was absorbed, a finger poked in his cheek, speed-reading the *Times*. He didn't notice me go by. He warmed up his brain on five or six newspapers every morning. I usually went through the two that were left on my desk each day, clipping out items for possible editorials. They were never used. Sandra and Jackie had each written an editorial while they were at Black Rock. I had to get one written too. My pride demanded it! I just hadn't been able to get one together yet, couldn't get my mind on it.

Joan Russell's office was next to Mike's. She waved, showing all her gleaming teeth. I waved back and continued on to my desk. Mannn, that Keating. Sure has got the bitches. I don't know what to think about him. Seems like he's stopped playing the role of great white father. Even calls me in to the staff meetings and asks me what I think about something, and listens to what I got to say. I don't know, maybe he ain't too bad a guy—kinda enjoy going out drinking with him too.

Betty, who was Mike's secretary and had her desk placed right behind mine, had her back to me, rummaging in the files. My eyes crawled over her tight yellow dress as I strode into the cubicle.

"Good morning, Betty."

She glanced up, smiling sweetly.

"Hi, Jimmy. I knew you were in. You left your attaché case on your desk."

"Yeah, that's to let the boss know I'm not late. He been asking for me?"

"No, not yet." She widened her smile, went over to her desk, and sat down.

I believe I was infatuated with Betty, but I never dared to let her know it, though sitting and breathing in her perfumed fragrance day after day I was sometimes tempted to. Betty was taboo. Betty was a beautiful white girl.

Yessss, Lord, there were a whole lotta fine white bitches swishing around Black Rock. They were nice to look at and some were very friendly. One was an outright cock-teaser!

Aileen had a greasy walk, everything on her just slid to me. My stomach grew warm when I saw her coming up the aisle heading toward my desk, and I pretended not to notice her approach, scribbling circles on a pad, cradling the telephone on my shoulder. A crisp voice spoke at the other end: "Board of Education, can I help you?"

"Yes, this is Mr. Watson of WCBS-TV Editorials. I'd like to speak to Mr. Rumley, please." Aileen was beside my desk now, speaking to Betty over the rapid tapping of her typewriter. I gripped the receiver tightly, holding her in the corners of my eyes as my guts began to slowly burn.

"I'm sorry, Mr. Rumley is away on vacation. Would you care to speak to Mr. Kraft, his assistant?"

"Yes, if you don't mind." Aileen's gray tailored skirt curved tight at the thigh as she swung a leg and draped a cotton-soft buttock over the edge of my desk. Blood rushed to my groin. She was sitting on my hand!

"Hold on, please. I'll try to reach him. Who did you say this was calling?"

"Mr. Watson of WCBS-TV Editorials."

"Thank you. Hold on please." I held on, staring coolly up at Aileen, her fluffed golden mane, tawny skin, gray cat eyes, sensuous mouth. Her beauty was beastly. She stirred, feeling the strength of my stare, then turned to meet it, interrupting her chit chat and licking her lips into a smile.

"How's it going today, Jimmy?"

"Good afternoon, Miss Thorp. You ever try to run down a fast-stepping bureaucrat by phone?" I stiffened my fingers under her ass.

"Oooooh, I don't envy you. That's a job." She was grinning fiercely, shifting her weight, pressing the fingers back down. "Believe me, I've tried it. Good luck." Her voice rose: "You make the wedding Sunday, Betty?"

The fucking wench. This makes the third time she's done that shit. What the fuck she messin' with me for? She got Tyrone sharing her office all day, or don't she go for yaller niggers?

Aileen squirmed, sending my knuckles right up the crack of her ass. I clenched my teeth, sucking in air. Uuuunnhh, BITCH! You cock-teasing dog! Why don't you do this to Al? You scareda that black motherfucker ain't yuh? Always running every time he put his rough black hands on yuh. He's too out in the open. He don't hide his shit. You like it sneaky, huh, bitch? I pinched at her panties.

"Hello, this is Mr. Kraft. Hello, anyone there?"

"Good afternoon, Mr. Kraft. This is Mr. Watson of WCBS-TV Editorials."

"Yes, how can I help you?"

"We're interested in finding out the number of community centers the Board of Education has currently in operation throughout the city." Aileen squirmed down harder. My nostrils flared drawing in her smell and my dick reared like an enraged animal kept from its prey.

"Oh, my, Mr. Watson, I don't have that information right at hand at the moment. I'll have to dig it up for you. How soon do you need it?"

"As soon as possible." Digging her claws into my shoulder for support, the vixen lifted her tail, freeing my hand, telling Betty she had work to do.

102

"Would you want that information broken down, day and evening, borough by borough?"

"If you don't mind."

"What say I mail this stuff to you in a day or two, okay?"

"That would be fine. Address it to Editorial Director, WCBS-TV, Fifty-one West Fifty-Second Street."

"—West Fifty-Second Street. All right, Mr. Watson, I'll get that to you as soon as possible. Thank you for calling."

The lying bastard. I had been trying to get that stuff from down there for over a week. They giving me the fucking runaround. Rumley said it was in the mail last Thursday. Well don't send the shit, motherfuckers. Keep on bullshiting. I don't give a damn if it gets here or not, I ain't calling no mo'. Fuck this editorial! If Mike want it he can get it hisself. That Aileen better quit bullshittin too, or I'm gonna crack on her for some of that pussy. Better not say no either. I'd kick her fucking ass. I'd beat that bitch into bad health! Ah-haaa! That would really fuck up Mike's program. Ol' Daniels would ram it up his butt: "You've got to take full responsibility for this mess, Mike. I went along with you because you assured me these niggers were tame. Now look what that buck of yours has gotten us into!"

Man, you crazy! Them Whiteys wouldn't let you get away with stomping that bitch. They'd put the police on your ass, and you know what that means:

"Good evening. This is the 'Six O'Clock Report' and I'm Jim Jensen. A huge, burly nigger was shot and killed by police this afternoon on the twenty-fifth floor of CBS corporate headquarters here in Midtown Manhattan. The dead nigger apparently went berserk during an attempt to ravish a lovely blonde CBS employee after she rejected his amorous advances. The slain coon was also employed by CBS. Police authorities are withholding the attractive victim's name and that of her fiendish attacker pending further investigation. We'll have a filmed report on the tragedy from Correspondent Chris Borgen after this message. . . . You mustn't try to fool Mother Nature. . . . And now a filmed report.

103

Authorities here say that during the voracious attack, the apparently sex-maddened nigger chewed unmercifully at his hapless victim, rendering deep gashes in her throat, ears, back, and breast. Doctors at St. Luke's Hospital, where the victim lies in critical condition, say it took one hundred and forty-two stitches to close the wounds. A coroner's report lists at least two hundred bullet holes in the dead nigger's carcass."

Man, you better not ask that white bitch for shit!

I often amused myself with thoughts like that, although, in reality, I was never afraid to hit on a white broad. No, it wasn't fear; white broads just didn't fit my image. I was on TV! TV, Daddy, and talking, so I believed, real black; seen each Saturday afternoon by my folks, friends, people at City College, by the black broads at CBS. Right on, Jimmy! Tell Whitey where it's at, baby. Power to the people, brother! The acclamations beat down on me like rain through a torn umbrella. I was a local celebrity; a new but small black voice. Hitting on white bitches would have blown that!

The dig *me* trip I was on, being a participant in a televised discussion group that mouthed off opinions on black attitudes toward white society, didn't last more than a couple of weeks. Everyone on the panel was black, and that made each of us an expert on black attitudes. As with all experts, we didn't always agree, but we disagreed courteously. Our differences increased as the questions became more complicated. Heated arguments flared up among us, with everyone trying to outblack the others. When this happened the producers and other big shots would say it was a good show. But I was beginning to hear criticism.

"Hey, man, how you gonna sit up there an say you don't mind if qualified white teachers teach in the black community? Is blacks gonna do the qualifying?"

"So you think it's all right for black and white to marry huh? WELL, you didn't say it was wrong!" I hadn't said it was right, either.

The black intellectuals on campus would chide me for

104

disagreeing with another black "in front of the man." I was not keeping a united front. And Alma said I should stop chewing gum. It made me ugly. And my mother called every week to say I should shave that mess off my face.

One Saturday after the show the phone rang. It was my father. After twenty years, it's him on the phone! He'd called to tell me that he had seen the program down at his local Republican clubhouse. In an almost sobbing voice, he said that I'd made him so proud in front of his Queens district leader and all his friends, he would be happy for the rest of his life.

His happiness ended when he called again, a short time later, and suggested that on my next show I say some crap about more young blacks should join the Republican Party. I refused. He got mad and hung up!

Criticism had been reaching the other panel members too. The word was out: White folks was laughing their asses off at us; we were funnier than "Amos 'n' Andy"! We was making other niggers ashamed. It had to STOP! An informal panel meeting was held: no more acting like fools, back to being courteous.

The producers didn't like that shit! Our program, they said, had become too "sterile," had lost its "spontaneity." The motherfuckers wanted to see us entertain; act the bone-in-the-nose nigger for twenty-five bucks a show; even dropped hints that if we got a little wilder they would consider giving us a raise and extending the program series. We stayed calm and took the chump change.

Meanwhile, over at Black Rock, I was having a different experience. Mr. Keating was not following the established CBS pattern: Apprentices should be displayed but not be given any independent responsibility. For some reason he wanted me to take my job seriously; get that editorial written; shoulder some responsibility and all that shit! The Lee Hanna and Harry Arouh incidents were still fresh in my mind. Besides, seventy-five bucks a week wasn't no driving force. He had to be nuts.

105

I kept giving him excuses. He kept on prodding. Then finally he summoned me to his office and asked me, "Jimmy, why can't you get a decent editorial together?" I couldn't tell him I didn't want to write it, that I was just hanging around until I could get me a steady connection. How could I tell this white man, to his face, this whole Apprenticeship Program was bullshit—and still keep the job?

"Well, Mike, it's like this. The editorial assignments you give me bore me. The way I have to go about getting information just doesn't work. It's a bitch to sit up here trying to get some information from somebody over the phone who don't want to give it up. I'm a outside guy. I'd rather git in the streets like a reporter an' find out things."

I was jivin', of course, never had it in my mind that he was gonna take me up on my suggestion. But damn if he didn't! He came from behind the desk and slipped into his suit jacket, then stood looking at me like he was thinking hard.

"Okay," he said, starting for the door. "I think it's a good idea. We'll talk about it Monday. Let's have a drink across the street tonight. Okay?"

"Okay with me."

Hanging out after work in the New York Hilton bar had gradually become a regular thing for me and Mike. Located as it was, just across Sixth Avenue from Black Rock, the Hilton bar was a convenient place for us both to talk, relax, get high—becoming slightly more intimate with each meeting.

I was sure those hours we had been spending in the bar influenced his decision, allowing me to go work out in the field unsupervised. It ain't so easy to go drinking with a guy half the night then the next day on the job treat him like a houseboy. The way I saw it, he was daring me to do a professional job. Shit or git off the pot! Well, I liked that kind of challenge!

One day, early in September, Mike invited Freddie Cole to hang out with us at the Hilton. Later that evening, after the three of us had put away a few rounds and our conversation had turned to broads, Freddie leaned closer to Mike as he raised his glass and asked,

"Have you ever been with a black woman?"

Mike's drink almost went up his nose! He hadn't been expecting that one. I hadn't either! I could feel his mind shaking off the alcohol. He lowered his glass slowly to the bar.

"What d'ya mean ever been with a black woman?"

"Have you ever *fucked* a black woman?" The coarse words rasped from Freddie's mouth and ground against the smooth, expensive atmosphere. Whatttt? Had this nigger gone CRAZY? I got both mad and embarrassed. If Mike was getting some black trim, I damn sure didn't want to hear about it!

Mike was hesitating, eyes coolly sizing us up. Then slowly his expression changed. He smiled blissfully.

"Ah yes, as a matter of fact—" Sandra! Sandra! I knew it! "—there was this black girl I met down in the West Indies." The black girl had been his first piece of tail. I listened in pain as Mike told his story, imagining every detail; his pale sweaty body slapping against her shiny black one, rooting up in her and then dropping his goddamn load in her—his stinking white sperm. THAT'S WHAT HAPPENED TO YO' MOMMA, FREDDIE!

I was going ape shit inside—Freddie was enjoying the story! He was grinning! The both of them were grinning. Freddie, you stupid ass, he's telling you how Whitey raped YO' MOMMA! . . . Goddamn you, Freddie! Why'd you have to come along? He and Mike knew how to talk . . . Freddie, you CAN'T talk that shit with no white man! Keatinggg, you fucking bastid! YOU BASTID! BOTH OF YOU FUCKIN' BASTIDS!

Mike pulled out a cigarette after ending his tale, checking reactions. Freddie gave him a light.

"You're from Canada, huh, Mike?" The boss blew out the smoke and smiled,

"Yes I was brought up in Montreal."

So you just had to confess, eh, boss? A niggeress took yo'

cherry. You jive-ass cracker. Break one a you Whiteys in on some black pussy an' you never forget it. Shame of yourself, motherfucker? You braggin' or what?

"—had a rough time getting my seaman's papers, but my father had this friend who was a—" Mike continued between gulps of whisky.

The conversation grew increasingly palsy, flooded with chuckles as the Cap'n and Freddie probed deeper and deeper into their pasts, exercising their brand new barroom brotherhood. I gritted my teeth. Freddie's white side was showing.

"Ever been up in Maine? Great country. I—" Mike's mouth had taken over completely now, full of reminiscences. "—we had this house on the beach—" Where do you get your black pee-hole now, Mr. Keating, 42d Street? "—we had these great lobster bakes . . . sometimes we'd spend the whole night out on the beach . . . with this big fire going—" I excused myself and went to the men's room.

Somebody liked Frank Sinatra. He was flying to the moon again when I came back. Mike was sailing his yacht. Freddie was sailing with him. I sat down wondering why my father had two half-white sisters.

"—I was out on Long Island Sound calling the Coast Guard for weather reports, calling another boat on my ship-to-shore radio like I was some Big Skipper . . . having a ball." He laughed. I cursed him silently, knowing he had a black maid. My grandmama had been a maid. My great-grandmama a slave. Fucking her, honky? Or do you cruise Southern Boulevard like the rest of the white creeps lookin' for a suck or a fuck from a two-dollar black junkie?

"—we'd have lunch at the Yacht Club. People there dress in white ducks and blue blazers—" Man, you white motherfuckers got everything. Cancha LEAVE OUR WOMEN ALONE?

Fortified by another round of drinks and encouraged by a spellbound Freddie, Mike went on and on. His episodes in the Canadian Navy. His rich businessman father. His mil-

108

lionaire car dealer brother. His ex-model, businesswoman wife.

"—Kathie runs her own PR ad agency—" This pampered motherfucker was making me sick. ". . . does quite well with it . . ." She know you dropped your first load in a dark hole? ". . . brings in fifteen, twenty grand a year . . . blah blah blah . . ." I drained my glass, fixing my eyes on him. Yeah, Keating, you one a them sick dick bastards. You been conned into thinking that white pussy of yours is sacred. DAMN FOOLS! Say you don't want us niggers mongrelizing your race but yet you sneak around slobbering after black pussy doing most of the MONGRELIZING yourself. You scared to come out in the open with your dark desires, huh, chump? If you did then maybe I could come out with my white ones. COME ON, MOTHERFUCKER, SAY WHAT'S INSIDE YOU.

"—Kathie's from a small town in upstate New York—" I know you can't admit it. You trapped man, just like me. You can't go against the white code shit. Your pure white pussy wouldn't be so sacred no more if you did. We both know it's all bullshit but we'll keep on playing the game until you Whiteys call it off for darkness.

The boss called for one more for the road. After it was poured, he produced his American Express Card and handed it to the bartender with a flourish. In the next second, before any of us had reached for his drink, Mr. White Knight suddenly laid out a royal invitation:

"Why don't you guys come up to my house next time. I'd like you to meet my family."

❊ ❊ ❊

Thursday evening a week later we were in a cab moving swiftly up Broadway after having a few rounds in the Hilton bar again. The gray light from a dying sun was descending on the city like a concrete mist that would soon harden into night. I sat in the back seat close by the window; Mike on one end, Freddie between us. Norman was up front next to the driver; he too had been invited to come along. Everyone was quiet. I gazed out through the open window, feeling the breeze against my face. Tree-studded islands, encrusted with mortar, glided past us as we headed uptown. Pedestrians strolled on crowded sidewalks beneath the tapering shadows of tall apartment complexes, out to shop, peat, take in a movie. We were on our way to Mike's crib.

I'd had time to think since accepting Mike's invitation. If he had come to my house I could have gained more prestige. Alma would have never stopped bragging. More important, I would have had him on my turf where I could have peeled his shell off. I'd-a tugged at that tight brain and studied his reactions (if that were possible; Mike rarely showed his reactions to anything). I had to know these things about him, things I couldn't find out in the Hilton bar.

In the honk of traffic, beating with the wind through the window, Mike's friendly invitation struck deep into my past:

("I want you should come up ta Wadder-berry when we get out, Jimmy—" I'd met Carmine in Marine boot camp and for four years we did almost everything together. He came home with me some weekends . . . dated the bitches around the block . . . ate, slept in my mother's apartment in the Bronx. We'd whored, drunk, and gambled together overseas.

("—yuh don't haf'ta worry 'bout nuttin', see? I got people dat's inta everythin'. Me and you gonna go inta bizness togedder, paisan. We like brudders."

(On a bright Sunday, years later, I pulled into a Connecticut gas station and phoned while Ava waited in the car with the kids. Carmine's wife asked me for my number at home, saying she'd have him call me. He didn't. I called three more times, and each time his wife said he wasn't in. And that ended that!)

110

8 The Puerto Rican doorman, dressed in a rotting grayish-blue uniform, leaped up from the imitation Louis XIV chair when he saw us coming and stood by the glass-paned entrance with a shit-eating grin on his face. He nodded to each of us as Mike led the way into the lobby and across its somber interior of faded marble to the elevator. A young, mod couple—the bitch was fat—were leaning against the opposite wall, chatting next to a broad mirror. I stared into it. In the gloomy light which drifted down from a dreary chandelier, four images were framed like a racial color chart—Mike white, Freddie beige, Norman brown, me black.

We stepped off the elevator at number 5. I was surprised that there was only one apartment off the small lobby. Damn, he must have twenty rooms in his. Mike passed Freddie the bag of liquor and unlocked the door.

"Come on in, gang. Eh, Kathie, I've got some of the gang with me."

I went in last and stood in the foyer, looking down a long hall. WELL, KISS MY ASS! Any ideas I had of swankness disappeared like a fart in a windstorm.

The place, despite its size, had a humble air. There were pious ancestral faces in gilt frames on the walls and dull

111

white paint; a small bookcase overflowing with paperbacks, a simple, inexpensive mirror, a skinny clothes closet, and a stained wood floor that needed covering. It resounded sharply under Mike's cracking heels as he marched down the hall. Big-time dude, I thought, following him.

We filed into a spacious living room, a clutter of Oriental rugs, English tapestry, and furniture from every period except the '60s. Big Daddy might have been makin' big cash, buying yachts and renting beach houses in Maine, but he wasn't spending shit on his New York apartment. Everything I'd seen in it looked handed down, excluding the woman. UNNN-HUNH!

She was sitting in a dark overstuffed chair across the room near a window. Her soft features had been burnished by the sun and were set in a regal expression. Small pearl earrings gleamed icily under her pale golden hair and the light blue minidress she wore had crawled up her thigh to a stop a shade shy of the danger point. She looked expensive and out of place in the old, high-ceilinged room, as if posing for *Harper's Bazaar* in a rummage sale warehouse.

"Kathie, I want you to meet some of the gang."

"Of course, dear."

Of course, dear. Humph. Ava never talked to me like that. Kathie rose with a dancer's grace, coming to meet us, smiling gently as we waited for the pleasure. I compared her velvet movements to Ava's pigeon-toed amble.

Mike eyed her until she paused a short distance away from us by a small coffee table, then he went to her, curling a possessive arm around her waist. I'd put my arm around a classy broad like Kathie once—at a millionaire's party out in Southhampton. I'd been hired, along with ten other muscle-bound dudes, to attend the guests; serving food, keeping the tables clean, shit like that. Man what a place and what fine-ass bitches! Rich folks damn sure looked different! I strode around like a black Mr. America, flexing my pec's, snapping Polaroid pictures of the guests at their request. I snapped one of the Gabor sisters. She flashed a stunning smile and

112

asked me to teach her the boogaloo. That was outa sight; me shaking ass with a Gabor. I left that party knowing I had to get rich someday. It felt sooooo good. I bet Kathie felt good too.

"This is my wife, Kathie."

I mumbled the fourth hello. I was careful how I looked at a white man's wife; looks could get a nigger into trouble— the worst kind! She was beautiful. Mike's manner became cocky, stiff with pride as he brought her closer, introducing us individually. How would he like it if a nigger took her away from him—bet he'd go crazy.

"This is Freddie— Oh, I'm sorry man. I'll take that." Freddie handed Mike the booze and nodded to Kathie. The word "man" had sounded awkward in his mouth. He was trying to sound hip; inserting a speck of blackness in his speech. Big phony!

"Norman and Jimmy." We dipped our heads slightly. Kathie widened her smile, curling her upper lip over a row of small, even white teeth. I saw her mouth quiver a bit at the corners, but Mike didn't notice. Was she nervous? We don't bite, baby, not in public anyway.

"Have a seat, gang. I'll fix the drinks. What are we having?" We'd started to sit and hesitated, "Scotch or wine?" His grin fastened on us niggers. Naturally we wanted scotch. Then to Kathie, who sang:

"I'll have some wine, Michael."

Now ain't that sweet? Ava called me Boobie. Shit!

"Anyone want ice?" Mike was strutting from the room, heading for the kitchen. We all wanted ice. Norman and me eased down into the love seat behind us. It looked frail and felt hard under my ass. Freddie dropped comfortably into an easy chair near Kathie's. She left the room, following Mike, probably to ask him what in the hell was going on! I slid away from Norman to the opposite side of the love seat, kicked one leg out and crossed it over the other. I was clean in a dark blue three-piece suit. Afro picked to perfection. I was ready! For what? I was sitting in a big-time Whitey pad. So what? I'd sat in his office chair, swiveled around, felt the power. Now I was in his house. I couldn't feel no power here, not like in Stan's house. This dude lived in a cave compared to Stan. Shit, Stan had real MONEY!

The scraping sounds of ice trays being torn from the refrigerator, water running, and cubes plunking in glasses escaped the kitchen above the distorted voices of the Keatings. The tone was light so I knew they weren't arguing. Maybe Lady Keating was making faces or frowns. I couldn't see from where I was sitting. What were they saying in there? And then the cold little spasms hit me, tightening the muscles in my belly. It was coming on again as it did whenever I entered Whitey's domain, his exclusive stores, his restaurants, his neighborhoods, his homes. The sickening fear of not being wanted.

Freddie looked across the room and grinned slyly. Norman's head was bowed, eyes fixed on the Oriental carpet. I guess he was thinking about his father who lay dying in Harlem Hospital. Why wasn't he there instead of here? Maybe he was curious like me. I lit up a cigarette, tossed the match in the ash tray on the coffee table and blew smoke Freddie's way, trailing it with a smile. What the fuck was he grinning about?

"Mother?" A young girl walked into the room, gave us a nonchalant glance and passed on into the kitchen.

"Mother?" She looked about eleven years old. That was the only childish thing about her. A minute or so later Kathie re-entered the room, holding a glass of wine, followed by her daughter, then Mike carrying a tray. He passed it around and we each took a glass. Now if he'd been at my house I would've brought out the bottle and let everyone pour his own. Naw, this liquor wasn't on the expense account; couldn't let these niggers drink up all his booze.

"Mother, where's the—" Over by the wall bookcase Kathie's daughter was speaking to her mother in a very mature tone. When she finished Mike motioned to her:

"Kara, I'd like you to meet the gang." Damn! Why did

114

we always have to be the gang—so he could be the fucking leader? She came to his side, observing us coolly. Damn! She was Mike and Kathie forged together; a sprinkle of freckles, light brown hair, glasses tipped on a pert nose. She looked to be near my daughter Yvette's age, but much more sophisticated and bolder—bet she knew all the right answers in school.

Mike waved his glass in our direction, and we nodded as our names were called: "Norman, Jimmy, Freddie, my daughter Kara." I wondered how she felt about three niggers being in her home. She said hello crisply and left the room. Mike sat down on a low sofa beside Kathie, and silence fell on the room like Mount Everest. Why didn't somebody say something. Come on, SAY SOMETHING!

"What do you have, Mike, two boys and two girls?" My voice was responding to Mike's piercing eyes. All right, Big Daddy, I'll start it off. I'd learned to tell by now when he wanted me to say something. He'd set the speed and direction. And if he started any of that shit about how much he liked black folks or how sorry he was for us, I'd get up and leave! Mike took a deep breath.

"Aaaaa, yes—" He brightened instantly. So did everyone. Kathie smiled at me like she was grateful I'd broken the silence. Yeah, baby, I ain't afraid to talk. Your man ain't the only man here.

"Young Michael attends school in Vermont. Kathie and I go up to visit . . ." As Mike continued speaking, three cats crept into the room, sniffing cautiously, checking us niggers out, one by one. Hey, man, does this dude have rats in his house?

". . . Neal's my youngest son, and—" I wished I had a son. I'd find a woman to give me one, but first I'd have to make some money; be a daddy for him to look up to.

"Kara's friends come around a lot—" Kathie nudged into the conversation, and the cats, satisfied we were harmless, began taking over, jumping on us and everything else.

". . . brings them home after school— Stop that! Get off

115

the table!—Oh, yes, it's a good public school, and the neighborhood's not too bad. Get down from there!" Shit, I had to go over to P.S. 99 last May about Yvette. Walked in that classroom and told them little sixth-grade black bastards: "THE NEXT TIME ANYONE A YOU THREATENS MY DAUGHTER WITH A KNIFE, I'M GONNA SHOVE IT UP HIS ASS!" The fuckin' teachers might be scared of 'em but I damn shore wasn't.

". . . yes, indeed, she's just like her father, that Martha. When she was . . ." The story Kathie told amused everyone; the first strains of laughter tittered around the room. I chuckled lightly. In the midst of it, Mike stood up holding his empty glass.

"Freddie, I see you need a refill. How about you, Norman? Jimmy?"

"Yeah, Mike, gimme some soda this time if you got it." The liquor was getting to me; my Whitey diction was slipping—better watch that shit!

"Alllll right. You guys want soda too? How about you, Kathie, more wine?" Freddie asked for soda, Norman had had enough. Kathie, her glass held to her lips, shook her head, "Uunnnh, no, dear." Just like the movies. Maybe if I asked her, she would give Ava a job at her office. Not now, later, if I got to know her better. Naw, I'd better put it to Mike first. Naw, Ava would fuck up; she never held a job. I didn't care; didn't want her working for Whitey anyway; rather put her in business for herself. One day. If she stopped fucking up; stopped being so damn frigid. Maybe when I made some money she'd change up. Was Kathie frigid?

Collecting our glasses, Mike left the room. The cats filed into the kitchen behind him, tails pointing straight up. I hoped they'd stay in there. The seconds passed while six eyes focused on Kathie. Although she and her husband were being excellent hosts, I still felt a wide and impassable something separating me from them. I wondered what the others were thinking.

"You know, on Sundays Michael prepares dinner for the

116

family," Kathie revealed in a voice he would be sure to hear.
"Can he cook?"

"Yes, I can, Freddie. You guys should come for dinner some Sunday and taste my specialty—roast beef, whipped potatoes . . ." For some reason my family never sat down at the table together. The kids ate in their room on TV trays, watching television. Ava took her meals late at night after I'd gone to bed. I always ate alone.

Kathie verified Mike's cooking as superb, then called to him sweetly. "Michael, you can bring me a piece of ice with you."

"I'll bring the whole tray," Mike said playfully.

"Oh Michael, I only want a piece."

"Okay, I'll bring you the wine too."

"Michael I didn't ask for—" And so the Keatings went on, jesting back and forth while Mike made the drinks. They sounded cute, young, real together. We niggers were laughing. I began to feel less and less suspicious.

Mike re-entered, walking around the room, passing the tray. He placed the wine bottle on the coffee table. Kathie smiled coyly, then laughed.

"For you, my dear." Mike dropped down beside her, smiling. I felt a twinge of envy. Kathie leaned across the table, picked up Mike's pack of cigarettes, and shook one out.

"My husband is very funny," she said teasingly, the cigarette crossed between her fingers. Mike struck a match for her. She inhaled deeply and exhaled slowly, pale blue smoke misting around her face. Her eyes met mine.

My infatuation with white women had been fostered mainly by the movies and the fact that white women were taboo. It had ended years ago, somewhere back in my early twenties. Until then, though, I'd hungered for them—Hedy, Gina, Brigitte, Marilyn, all had writhed beneath me, screaming in frenzied ecstasy: "Aaaayiiiii Poppeee—I LOVE IT— I LOVE YOUUUU! Oooh, shit. JIMMY, DARLING!"
—and I'd wake up ejaculating thick, rich sperm. At thirteen the movies had me convinced: If God had made anything

117

better than a white woman, he'd kept it for himself. (Well, didn't white bitches belong to demigods anyway?)

Crossing Prospect Avenue one childhood day in front of a black Caddie I saw a big, black, hog-faced, processed-head nigger sitting behind the wheel. He jerked a cigar angrily from his mouth and slapped the shit outa the woman sitting beside him. She shrieked in pain, then threw herself on him, covering his faces with kisses. "Oh Daddy, I'm sorreee." HOLY SHIT! The woman was fine, blonde, and WHITE! I LOVED IT—promised myself I'd get to do that shit someday.

So I went up to Montreal and shacked up for eleven months, free of charge, with two fine-ass, high-class French-Canadian whores who only served judges and government officials. I released every movie fantasy I had. I gorged myself and found that I was empty. Why did they stink? They farted and shitted and menstruated, looked different in the morning, not at all like my Hedy or my Gina or my Marilyn. My dreams shattered, I came back home.

Mike blew out the match and said: "You know, Jimmy's married and has two kids."

Kathie's eyes held mine. "Oh, do you, now?"

"Yeah, he's the old man in the SEEK program. His kids will be sitting in college with him before he graduates."

Everyone laughed. It seemed, at least on the surface, that all the tension was gone. I lifted my glass, taking small sips, and began to paint a beautiful picture of my lovely family; the kids, my wife, the things we did together, where we traveled, lying my ass off. The Keatings sitting there together, so secure, so poised, so much how I desired Ava and me to be, believed me. Me and my family never did a damn thing together any more. Ava cooked, drank beer, and hated to give me pussy. My kids were being pounded daily with that no-good-nigger-man shit and slapped with "I'll tell your Daddy to beat you if you do that again."

I was the Beast that Beats. Now that was really a mother-fucker, 'cause I never laid a hand on them. It was a different story when it came to all the blood niggermen in Alma's family; they had good jobs, cash, homes. They were successes, they were praised!

I was doing everything I knew to make the grade—college, CBS. I wanted to belong to MY family, to be loved and accepted. Humph, to them I wasn't shit. I envied Mike! I hated the motherfucker! I felt an urge to ask him what I was doing wrong. Fuck it! White man always telling me what I'm doing wrong. I'M BLACK AND I AIN'T GOT NO MONEY, THAT'S WHAT'S WRONG!

Why'd I like Mike?

"Come in here." Mike noticed the dark woman and waved to her in a debonair manner, drawing everyone's attention to her standing in the doorway. He was feeling his liquor.

"Bessie, I want you to meet some of my friends." Damn! He sure was taking a lot for granted.

Bessie came around to the front of the love seat; eyes seeming to gauge us niggers' faces, weighing them against the Keatings'. She stopped near Mike and hunched into herself, trying not to take up too much space.

"Hell-low," she muttered. We returned her greeting. Mike moved closer to her; for a second I thought he was going to sling his arm around her. He didn't. The broad was over forty and just under ugly.

"Bessie's been with us for years." The statement implied Bessie had attained semifamily membership. She grinned house-nigger style. She had a right to be glad. She wouldn't a made it anywhere else with that face. The Keatings probably weren't paying her very much. Still holding her grin, Bessie excused herself properly and scurried off. Mike watched her leave, smiling affectionately.

When she'd gone, he turned to us,

"Eh, guys, let me show you the house."

After the tour was over, we settled back down in our seats. Through the curtains, Manhattan lights dotted the dark. It was time to leave.

119

"Anyone care for another drink?" Mike looked about ready for the nearest bed. I got up to leave.

"No thank you, Mike, it's a long ride uptown. Got to get up in the morning. Work, you know." Mike laughed and walked along with me as I started down the hall, his wife, Freddie, and Norman behind us. At the door we all said goodby, and the Keatings welcomed us to come again—just like we were old friends. Did they mean it? Why would he want to be friends with me? Did he feel threatened in his world and in need of some people who couldn't threaten him, people he could feel superior to? Is that why we were invited? Naw, I didn't think so; he could do that all day at the office. Maybe he was just tired of playing Big Man twenty-four hours a day; he hadn't acted Big Man while we were here.

Later, riding a rumbling subway uptown to the Bronx, I thought more about the visit. Mike had gone out of his way to be friendly. Didn't he realize we could never really be friends? I liked him well enough, but that was a long way from trusting him. He seemed a little too anxious for us to see his style; for me more than the others. So he had a yacht, sent his kids to good schools, took his family to Maine each summer. So what? In his home I saw just how little the Big Man was; he was just an ordinary dude caught up in the jaws of everyday living, being consumed by his job and the pretense that he was important—I got the feeling he knew it.

I didn't want to be no Cronkite. I didn't want to be no Keating either. I didn't want to waste my time any more thinking about becoming something big in the white folks' world. I was thirty years old. I was thinking about cash. Lay some cash on me and I'd be dynamite. Big-time Jimmy Watson.

Still, Mike and I experienced life from different positions on the tree. He was up top, I was below. Well, he had his and I'd damn sure get mine. When I did I'd come back to see him. Maybe then we could be friends. I kinda hoped so. The guy was all right in his way. He'd hear about

120

me one day, I was sure. I was gonna be big-time Jimmy Watson. I KNEW IT!

*　*　*

Stan dropped by my house in the Bronx with two shopping bags filled with cash. Man, I had never seen, known, been near that much money in my life. My breath came in short, quick gasps and my heart boomed inside my chest when he dumped the bulging bags on my living room floor. Stacks of money—hundreds, fifties, twenties, tens in neat bundles held together with rubber bands. They tumbled softly onto the stained, dirty gray carpet and lay in a haphazard heap.

"Go 'head an' pick some up." Stan stood over the pile of money urging me to touch it, to feel what it was like to have that much money in my hands.

I did! I picked up armfulls of it, then dropped it back on the worn carpet, then grabbed another armful and threw bundles up in the air, watching them hit the ceiling and fall back with a muffled thump. I pitched some to Ava sitting on the sofa, and like a basketball player she caught bundle after bundle and dropped them in her lap.

YEEeeeOOWWWeee!

The feeling was almost maddening. What I could do with this! God damn! Shitttttt!

Ava sat there, lap full of cash, grinning her ass off. This is what she wanted. This would make her happy!

Stan: black wide-brim hat, high black leather boots, full-length gray Persian lamb coat opened to show his black nylon jumpsuit. He stood there, hands on his hips, smiling, taking it all in.

I looked at Stan. "Is it real?"

"Sho, motherfucker." He frowned. "Is it real? Is pig pussy po'k?"

A month later I quit CBS and became a pusher in Stan's family.

121

9 When I walked into the office that morning the atmosphere was fluttering with small-craft warnings. A familiar feeling. Someone was going either up or out.

"Lee Hanna's been fired." It was the first news of the day my assistant presented me after I had opened the *Washington Post* and put two bags of sugar in the coffee my secretary had brought.

So he had lost. Hanna had been struggling against it for the last six months. A change of general managers had brought in a Hanna critic, who had been after him.

I had been observing the battle, been participating in it subtly. Hanna and some of those who worked for him had called a meeting some time before, where they challenged the stance I had taken editorially in support of the black activists attempting to decentralize the New York City school system. Hanna and company had presented a case to the General Manager, saying, in effect, that I was ignorant on the subject. To me that was a clear signal from Hanna that it was going to be either me or him at WCBS-TV, that we no longer could coexist.

I had tried to be a noncombatant in the incessant warfare

at WCBS-TV, but I had discovered that at certain times gauntlets were flung, and when that occurred it was either bite or be bitten. He had bitten, and any time I was asked my opinion of Hanna's work as News Director I bit back. He was accused of running an overly expensive operation and producing a news product that was too slick and shallow. I rarely disagreed.

Few people got any work done on the twenty-fifth floor that day. The office was a flush of excited gossip about the reasons for Hanna's firing and speculation as to his successor.

His firing was not a surprise to me or, I suspected, to Hanna. The General Manager had been calling me into his office during the last four or five days to ask my opinion of this candidate and that candidate for Hanna's job. He had put out the word that he was looking for a new News Director, and the applications were flooding in, some of them from within CBS itself. Hanna must have known what was going on. He always had been among the first to know who was getting whose job. His intelligence apparatus was consistently good.

In the afternoon, the General Manager poked his head inside my office.

"Come on down to my office, will you?"

When I went in, he said, "Well, you've heard what happened with Lee?"

"Yes, I heard."

"We talked about our disagreements yesterday and he wasn't going to change. He had to go."

"Yes."

The General Manager began a rambling discussion about the various candidates for the job. Then he looked sharply at me:

"How would you like to be News Director?"

I had not expected that. I had no managerial experience, and the News Director supervised an operation of 160 people and an annual budget of $5 million plus.

123

"Take a little time to think it over, Mike. But I need your answer this afternoon."

Back at my office, I ran the situation through my mind, examining, weighing, wanting to make the right decision. There were negatives. Becoming News Director would take me further away from the work that made me happiest, writing and reporting. Nothing at CBS, for instance, had given me as much satisfaction as my work at the *Herald Tribune*—a roving correspondent between the State Capitol in Albany and the Republican national primaries around the country. As News Director my work would be totally executive—no more writing, no more on the air, no travel, little free time. And, of course, it was full of peril. Hanna's predecessor had been fired too. If I took the job I would be next. The News Director was held directly responsible for the news programing that every executive in the company and their friends watched. There were too many critics and too little power in the job to enable one to survive very long. I had never been fired from a job. How would I stand up to it?

But there were positive aspects too. It would end the suffocating regularity of those 5 P.M. tapings, Monday through Friday, rain and shine. It would restore my privacy. No need to respond to strangers any more. I would not have to have an opinion on everything. And I would be in charge of the biggest and best local TV news operation in town. Plenty of talent and plenty of money. I could practice journalism to the utmost of my capacity. The General Manager knew the type of hard-edged journalism I was committed to, so presumably he would support me when push came to shove with higher echelons in the company. It certainly would happen, just as it had been happening in my editorial work. And it probably would end the meaninglessness I was sensing about my present work. I had visions of great broadcasts, ones that would push into the real life of the city and startle the audience with their gritty truth. Yes, it would be exciting, something I should do, if only for the experience. Who cared what happened in the end? Take a taste! And the job carried an $8,000 raise.

* * *

The News Director had to be within reach of the newsroom at all times to make the decisions that news events compelled. The assignment desk had to have my permission to keep crews on overtime or to roll the expensive mobile units to the scene of a news event; I had to mediate disputes, to rule on sensitive material being considered for broadcast, to answer the questions posed by corporate heavies about our broadcasts. If I needed to sneak away without leaving telephone numbers I took along a beeper, an electronic paging device that went off with a shrill whine anywhere in New York whenever the office wanted to speak with me. I wore the beeper on my belt, except when I took off my pants. Then I kept it on the floor if she didn't have a table near the bed.

There were three television sets in my bedroom at home —one for CBS, one for NBC, and one for ABC. When the 11 o'clock news came on, I would watch the three sets simultaneously, making notes on the comparative performances for next day's analysis and smoking a joint. Within five minutes of the end of the broadcast, the General Manager would call me to deliver his critique of the show and ask questions. My wife would fall asleep while I was talking to him.

Getting away for weekends—skiing in the winter, swimming in the summer—became increasingly difficult to do. There were shows to watch during the weekend, decisions to be made, questions to answer. Occasionally I would travel within on the weekend, discovering the marvels of myself and other dimensions of the world, a new perspective opened to me by LSD. I wanted to learn more, but there was little time. Isolation was needed for a good trip, and I had little of that.

125

Every now and again, Jimmy Watson would call. Out of the blue.

* * *

Stan had passed the word: No more operating; everybody take a vacation. Dynamite! I flew down to Acapulco for a couple of weeks, came back—no action. I jumped back on a plane and lay in Haiti almost a month, came home—still no action.

I began to get restless; dudes all around me were making cash. Shit, I had just started making some real money when Stan called a halt. That shit was all right for him, Andre, and Bama—them niggers had plenty scratch!

The dudes that worked for me all was crying the blues. They needed some merchandise; the high cost of living was still going on. And so was the high cost of being a boss: Niggers looked to me to solve their problems, and I, like a fool, thought that I could.

It wasn't hard to make direct contact with the Wops. In a few days I was rolling again, in a few weeks I was making a whole lot of money. The Wops were giving me dynamite heroin. Now was the time to get rich! RICH! I got together all the cash I could and copped—big!

I poured out drugs to dudes on consignment. Get rich! Then the reports started to come in. "The thing is falling off. . . . The stuff is garbage." The drugs were synthetic. The word was out on the streets: Jimmy's shit ain't no good! And the niggers who owed me was spending my cash somewhere else. Motherfucker, I was losing my ass off!

I called Nick, the Wop I had given my money to. He listened and said he'd make things right. He'd call me. Two weeks went by. I called again. He said: "Don't call no more!"

The fuck'n Wop bastard. He wasn't gonna get away with that shit! I'd rat the motherfucker out. How? Mail an anonymous letter? No. A reporter? A reporter! Inside story and all that shit. Fuck 'em up! Fuck 'em uppp, baby! Call Keating. Yeah, that's it! Call Keating—

❀   ❀   ❀

It was about 2:30 when I saw Mike's figure emerge from Broadcast Center striding confidently. I felt good knowing such a powerful representative of the white world, personally. He could make things happen. So could I! All it had taken was a phone call and here he was meeting me—Jimmy the hustler. Dig that shit.

He caught sight of my car and leaned forward slightly to see if it was me behind the wheel. I started the engine and he climbed in beside me.

"Hi there."

"What's happening, my man?" I grinned, pulling off. "Where to?"

"I don't know. Want to go to a bar on the East Side? Is that cool for you?"

"It's cool."

I glanced at Mike from time to time as we talked and rode crosstown. He was talking light, being cool but friendly. We hadn't seen each other in years. I wondered how he was digging my new style, the leather clothes I had on, my Caddie.

We had spoken very briefly over the phone. I might have a story for him, I said, a drug story. Now that we were together I had doubts. I'd have to tell him I was involved in drugs. What did he think about drug dealers—could I trust him not to implicate me?

"Gino's is in the next block."

We walked in and sat down at a small table up front beside a wide window that looked out on the traffic. What if I had been followed? I was nervous; what I was planning to do was dangerous. I was getting ready to RAT! I dillydallied around a while, making up my mind while we talked. Then in a hushed voice I began to tell Mike my plans to bust the Wops.

I gave him license plate numbers, phone numbers, locations, and some names. I felt strong as I rapped. I could lay something on them bastards and they wouldn't know where it came from. Jimmy Watson knew people, goddammit!

I finished rapping and paused, waiting for Mike to say something. He sat stroking his chin, his eyes fastened on mine.

"Why do you want to do this?"

Shit! I hadn't thought he'd ask that! Suddenly I felt like a punk.

"Er . . . well . . . er. I'm getting out of the business, but I got to stop those guys."

"Why?"

"Well, I found out they're selling to kids, putting shit in the schools."

It sounded weak. Mike didn't look like he believed me. He just kept staring into me. After a few moments he said:

"Well, I could get in touch with Burton Roberts—"

Mike was sidestepping me. The DA's office. Never!

"I don't know if that's such a good idea. He might wind up busting me too."

"He won't have to know about you." Shit, all I wanted was for Mike to tip the feds and write the story. Wasn't that what he wanted, the big drug story? I didn't want nothing to do with Burton Roberts!

"I'll think it over, but if you could handle it another way, I think it would be better."

"Why?"

"Just a hunch." Shit, them Wops could find out anything they wanted to in New York City—even who tipped the DA. That was out!

"Hey man, when's the last time you had a bitch suck cocaine off you dick?" I changed up, letting the tension off. I'd been flirting with my life a few seconds ago. Now I was smiling into the delights of the hustler's life: the girls, the cocaine parties, travel. Then I flashed my bankroll on him, proof that I was living high, riding around with $1,500 on me. This dude had to understand how for real it was to hustle, to take chances, to feel how alive it was, how rewarding it was. I wanted him to know that my life now was just as good as his, maybe even better! He had to dig that I was something now! Where would I have been if I had stayed at CBS?

"Whatcha feel like doing, man?" I flashed him a broad grin.

"I don't know," he perked up, "what're you up to?"

"Let's hang out—I'll get you a girl."

"Sounds great to me."

❋ ❋ ❋

The first break in the daily routine usually came around 11 o'clock in the morning. The mail was handled by then, the errors, miscues, the sloppy performances from the newscasts of the night before had been discussed, delegated, and chastised, and there was time at 11 o'clock to leave my office in the corner of the building and stroll through the newsroom saying hello, checking with the desk in the center of the room on the day's coverage of events in New York, congratulating a cameraman on the quality of his footage on the "Eleven O'Clock News" of the night before, and not, of course, forgetting to say a word to those who were spreading the accusation that the boss was getting out of touch with the troops, isolating himself in his office, the only one in the WCBS-TV News Department with a device that closed the door electromechanically, activated by a button on the underside of the desk.

And, yes, the button had become polished with use. The times were tense then at CBS. Cigarette advertising was going off the air by decree of the government, the recession was getting deeper each week, and station revenues, as well as most other revenues of the corporation, were falling and falling. Chairman Paley was stamping his foot, demanding that the downward trend be halted and reversed. The orders came down the line—chairman to president to divisions to units: Cut the budget!

At WCBS-TV the biggest budget was that of the News Department. Twice a week at least I would press that button to close the door on yet another long, tedious session with news executives, analyzing line by line each expenditure, looking for cuts that could be made without imperiling the stations's ratings—tops at 6 P.M., second at 11—and avoiding wholesale firings of those ambitious people I said hello to each day at 11 o'clock. But the operational savings we eventually devised were not enough; the company's revenues still did not provide a big enough growth of profits, it was decreed, and eventually the further order came: "The savings are not enough. The Chairman wants bodies."

And so we began to prepare lists of people to be fired, and just about every day calls came from my superiors. "How many bodies can you give us?" Lists of people who could be discharged were prepared all over the company and sent upward to the Chairman.

And those telephone conversations were always conducted behind the closed door. The signals of trouble were up throughout the company, and the energies of many of the news staff were being expended on eavesdropping on conversations in my office and upside-down surreptitious reading of confidential memos freshly opened on my secretary's desk. Everyone wanted to know whether they would be on the street. It was not a happy prospect. All of the stations were undergoing similar stresses and were laying off personnel.

There were private tensions as well. In the fear-filled atmosphere of the budget crisis, an ideological struggle was going on.

At 11 o'clock I was in the newsroom chatting with the day assignment editor when Beverly came down the corridor, her brown eyes flicking over the open room cluttered with

130

desks, telephones, and film crews awaiting assignments, looking for me. A friend, an ally who worked across Manhattan in the CBS headquarters building, was on my phone in my office. He had been calling me almost daily in the last few weeks, giving me the daily battle reports, the ideological battle reports.

This type of struggle was not new to me—I had fought plenty of ideological battles in the five years I was Editorial Director—but the dimensions were new. First of all, the right-wingers within the company had joined ranks and were asserting themselves more aggressively since Nixon had taken office and Agnew had started threatening the media. Although Frank Stanton continued to make his traditional speeches criticizing government encroachment on freedom of speech, beneath him were a growing number of wealthy executives who agreed with Agnew that the problem with America was what the people were being told. They were manning their barricades.

In addition, there was a general panic in the company in reaction to the Washington pressure and the sour mood being exhaled from Paley's office because of the declining revenues. In the scrambling about to lay blame for the fiscal problem, rising corporate stars were yanked from their jobs and told to look for employment elsewhere. It was genteel enough on the surface. They were given a desk and a secretary but no function while they tried to find new jobs. People at lesser levels were just kicked out.

The type of news broadcast I had initiated since becoming News Director had been stirring opposition in the troubled suites across town.

We had broadcast a documentary on the rioting city prisons sympathetic to the embittered blacks and Puerto Ricans locked in prison unable to raise bail and not convicted of any crime. We had looked into profit-taking on Wall Street, wondering how come the fat cats continued to make money during the recession while the small investors lost their Arrow shirts. We had broadcast a daily series explaining the benefits, dangers, and harm of the variety of popular drugs consumed by Americans, concluding that alcohol was more personally and socially destructive than marijuana.

Memos had been arriving from across town asking what was going on—why was the news on WCBS-TV so "one-sided"? In their minds our broadcasts seemed to be contributing to what they saw as a general disintegration of the country.

I entered my office, got behind the desk, glanced briefly at the three TV monitors on the far wall, and picked up the phone.

"Can you talk?"

"Yes." And I pushed the button closing the door.

"Start looking for another job. They're going to get you this time. I just came from a meeting."

Rumors of this had been around the company for months, but then they were always around. The local News Director was always on the edge of the abyss, never lasting in the job long enough to gather sufficient power of his own with which to defend himself. The certainty of being fired went with the job. The moment appeared to be at hand.

So there was no shock, no shattering of glass within me at his words. But then the conviction enveloped me that my friendly informant was in reality, oh, yes, turning on me and was now playing the game of my enemies. Even he. And the desperate tension of being alone and unprotected against the new group in the corporation nervously rattling their power flickered through the muscles of the back of my neck, causing a knot on the left side behind the ear to which I was holding the phone. At that moment I believed my friend was ingratiating himself with the new power group by trying to scare me out of the company, getting me to leave on my own initiative. That would spare everyone the risk of a public squabble should they just fire me straight out. There would be questions—one of them would be about the role of the Catholic Church, which had mounted a furious protest against a broadcast illustrating the ease with which a

132

woman, a Catholic woman, had obtained an abortion in New York. The bishops had ordered Sunday sermons by the parish priests in the three states of the New York metropolitan area, and the priests had urged the parishioners to write, and the letters had poured in. And there were, to be sure, the personal phone calls from the clergy to their communicants within the upper reaches of the company. A right reverend monsignor whom I knew slightly had called me the morning after the broadcast, opening the conversation with:

"I hear you broadcast a murder last night."

The vigor of the Church's attack had sent a wave of fright undulating through the company. Preparations were made for what was expected to be a summons from the Federal Communications Commission. Many of those who wrote to CBS noted that they had also written the FCC. Lawyers from the CBS Law Department were sent to the News Department to prepare what was to be a defense of the broadcast and the personnel who had produced it should an FCC hearing result. After the lawyers had been in the News Department a week, the chilly realization formed among us that the lawyers' real object was not a defense of the broadcast and its personnel but a prosecution. Should CBS be summoned to Washington because of the abortion story, the company would disassociate itself from the broadcast, and the careers of those associated with it would be ruined.

I was astonished and embittered by the company's plan and ultimately disgusted when the request came from the terrified new General Manager of the station that I fire the correspondent who reported the abortion story. I refused, and that brought on a flexing of strength between me and the new leaders of the Television Stations Division. They backed off that time, but it was not forgotten and was mentioned every now and again when new conflicts arose.

"Well," I told my friend across town on the telephone who was telling me that the end was near, "I'm going to have to think about that. I don't know right now what I'll do."

133

Not going to let him detect my reaction, unsure whether I had pierced all the levels of his motivation. Perhaps his game was more complex than I perceived. He was a clever man.

"I'm thinking about you in this," he went on, excited, urgent, and friendly. "You'll have a better chance at another job now than after you've been canned. Listen, Mike, they're going to do it. You're not going to win this time. Believe me. Call that friend of yours at NBC. See what they've got over there."

"Thanks. I appreciate your letting me know."

I hung up the phone bleakly, my mind beginning to race with alternatives. Call the guy at NBC; kiss ass with the new centurions of CBS and promise to make nary a wave that might penetrate the worried consciousness of the established power in New York; manipulate my way around my enemies, now that I had advance knowledge of their plans; or just continue on, letting events take their course, saying nothing and permitting the special reporting unit to go on shaking things up, as it was doing every fortnight now.

But after less than a year on the job—my mind was racing faster now—I felt the balance tipping. The fun was souring. It was supposed to have been my most satisfying journalism trip. But the executives who had appointed me and had been supportng me had been fired. The budget was being cut. Much of the staff was nervously hostile to change, and my energies were being drained by meaningless internal corporate squabbles instead of journalism. So what was this new struggle all about in the end? Was there a victory worth seizing? Would not one increasingly dreary struggle inevitably lead to another and another, having no meaning other than the struggle itself, ending only upon retirement or death?

My thoughts stepped then onto a different plane. Why did I believe my friend across town was playing double agent? A man who had been the straightest with me of everyone

134

at CBS, who genuinely liked and admired my work, and I his. What was going on in my head?

Oh, yes, it started rolling in now, like the ninth wave. No trusting anyone any more, even the man who moments ago in an act of friendship had risked his own career by telling me of the secret machinations against me. He wasn't stabbing me in the back. It mattered to him that I had a wife, four children, and no stock options. He was grasping my shoulder and acting as a friend. I realized then that I was frightened.

Jesus Christ, I was scared!

So, Keating, this is the kind of shit you've been passing off to yourself as a life. A transition from joy to fear, a vigorous run down the incline.

Get off this dungheap, man, before you become a knifeblade, trembling there, waiting for your next target, your next protective reaction strike, spending your energies, your human glory, protecting your ass!

And I decided then that I would take no steps to arrest the actions that were in motion, that the situation in which I had placed myself would arrive on its own momentum to its own conclusion—that I would go down in flames and dance in their light.

✿ ✿ ✿

From the *New York Times,* December 18, 1970:

"Michael F. Keating was dismissed yesterday as news director of WCBS-TV. He was replaced by Ed Joyce, a radio newsman for the station's parent company, the Columbia Broadcasting System.

"The unexpected announcement was made here by Robert L. Hosking, who took over as Channel 2's vice president and general manager on September 28. It comes at a time when Channel 2 is locked in a fierce three-way battle with WNBC-

TV and WABC-TV for the rating leadership on the 6 and 11 P.M. news reports.

"Mr. Keating, who declined to speculate on the reasons for his dismissal, did say that he thought they had nothing to do with the ratings situation. 'As a matter of fact,' he said, 'the station is going ahead with the format changes I initiated.'

"Asked to comment on Mr. Keating's removal, Mr. Hosking said:

"I simply felt that Ed Joyce is a stronger manager than Mike by virtue of experience. However, I feel there is a real place for Mike Keating in our organization and hope to utilize him in the future.'

"Mr. Keating has been asked to remain with CBS but Mr. Hosking could not say yesterday where he might be employed. It was understood that Mr. Keating had the option of working in management or in the news area.

"The former news director, who had assumed the post last April, said he planned to take a short vacation and decide on his future when he returns."

Before the skiing vacation I went to the News Department's Christmas party atop the Pan Am building despite the announcement of the day before. I didn't have to go, but I thought I would. For the occasion I wore a tie with the signs of the zodiac and the colors of psychedelia. I wasn't going to a funeral. It felt more like a birthday party, and my wife gave me a look of admiration as I left the apartment for the party.

10 I was grinning my ass off riding in Stan's big new hog. More feel, more sound, more life in that bad, mean motherfucker than in your own living room. We was riding down Grand Concourse smoking reefer. Some hip Willie Bobo on Stan's tape deck had me and was tearing me up. The car was riding so smooth and the tape was socking Latin so mean that when we hit an occasional bump it felt like it came out of the rhythm section.

It was early afternoon, nice, sunny spring day, not too cool. Not many girls strolling the Concourse, too early. But, shit, I was digging the car.

We swung right on 149th Street and on across the 145th Street Bridge into Harlem. The light caught us at Seventh Avenue. Stan had heard about some bad smoke some dude from the Dominican Republic had downtown on the West Side, in the 70s. We wanted to cop.

Stan turned to me while we were waiting for the light.

"You know, man, how the fuck you gonna be happy with no money? You ever see a broke motherfucker happy? I ain't. Not here in America. Shit, not anywhere. Let a guy find out what money is, an' he ain't never gonna be happy till he git some."

137

I pulled up on the joint as the car moved off.

"You goddamn right."

Stan was the boss, the sun in our solar system. Personality, charm, looking like a darker Harry Belafonte—and brains! God, did he have brains! And clean, too. When I first met him back in '65 he was dressing his ass off, outa Leighton's and Phil Kronfeld's, the best. And sitting in his car five years later he was still cleaner than the Board of Health. In five years he'd come from a good hustler to the boss of hustlers, formed into families, Mafia style. Drugs was his business. I was his cousin's lieutenant, but I was boss of my own family. The Wops gave it to Stan, and through him all the families were supplied.

When he had stopped over at my place in 1968 with the shopping bags full of cash, he didn't say how he got it and I didn't ask. He did say I could make that kind of cash, and more. When I was ready, let him know.

Yeah, baby, he'd left it like that. When I was ready.

There I was with bills up to my scalp, a wife, two kids, paying rent, going to school, working for CBS during the summer makin' nothing but carfare, lunch, and cleaner's bills, going into my thirties, and broke. But I didn't want money that way, illegally. How 'bout that shit?—I didn't want that kinda money. It wasn't long before I wanted any kinda money. Money ain't bad. In fact, money is damn good. Just imagine that: Whitey had trained me to where I thought something was bad about money you hadn't gotten the way he says it's all right to get it!

❖   ❖   ❖

The Funky Inn was an after-hours joint in an apartment —a place to gamble, pull on reefer, snuff up coke, guzzle booze, meet pussy, and possibly get killed! I was the cocaine man and The Inn was one of my main stations. I could pull in about five hundred long ones each Friday and Saturday night after the bars closed. My routine was to pass a

138

forty-dollar spoon around the gambling table to get the niggers open, walk out into the bar-parlor, and order a scotch
and soda that I'd sip on while I checked out the pussy. It
wouldn't be long before "Eh, Jimmaaaaay" rang out from the
gambling room.

It was also a practice of mine to set out a twenty of cocaine on the bar to warm up the stray pussy that was always
stuck to the bar stools or poured over the lounging sofas at
either end of the booze station. They waited in ambush for
the winning cocks to come out and stiffen in their direction.
None of them bitches ever offered to buy, so it was simply
a case of goodwill with me or sometimes an investment in
a future fuck.

It was after I'd done my routine, waiting to be summoned,
decked out in a tight, handmade, bell-bottomed jumpsuit
open from my neck to my belly button, that I felt a soft tap
on my shoulder. I turned holding my liquor glass between
my thumb and forefinger, pointing a diamond-belted pinky
to where the tap came from. There she was. Pepper!

"You got a spoon?" She sounded hip but sweet.

"I got whatever you want!"

"What it cost?"

Now I thought she was trying to get slick. Anybody that
buys coke knows the price.

"Forty dollars!" I sounded a little nasty. If the bitch wanted
a free sniff she could have it. Wasn't no sense in bullshitting
that she wanted to buy a spoon.

"Can I taste it?" She looked almost scared.

Now I was sure the bitch was begging. All the local hustlers
knew that I had the best blow around. I copped straight from
a South American dude who flew out of the country and
brought it back himself. I fished down into my silk jockey
drawers with my left hand, still holding my drink with my
right, where I kept a small stash wrapped in aluminum foil
knotted up in a handkerchief. I came out with it and undid
the knot with one hand.

"Here, baby!" I palmed a twenty and tucked it in her

139

hand, twisted the handkerchief into a ball that I sent diving
back down in my crotch in one swift unbroken movement.
I dismissed her like a misdemeanor, turning my back and
aiming my jeweled pinky finger to the roof, slowly dumping
the scotch down my mouth.

I'd said "Here, baby" so loud everybody would know that
she was begging!

My play had been so strong that if she had been with a
man he would have to give her money to cop something off
me. If he didn't, everyone would know that he was on his
ass, resorting to steal-dog methods to get a high. But if she
didn't have no man, she owed me some ass, any way that I
wanted it—with my foot or my plugging stick. Either way
it went I couldn't lose. I had plenty of coke.

I forgot about her as Rocky the bartender poured me a
drink on the house. He expected a free sniff. Rocky was
pouring me another house drink when I felt her touch on
my shoulder again. I turned to see her standing, left hand
gripping her hip, forming a triangle under her left arm.
Her mouth spit acid:

"Here's yo' twenty!" peeling a Jackson off a thick roll. Now
she was talking loud, "And fix me up a half-a-quarter," snatching four more Jacksons from the green ball she had, pushing
them at me like a pro.

I locked eyes with her, crumpling her cash in my fist. I
liked this bitch. She had class, too much for this kinda joint.
I called off the war with a smile and she agreed with one
of her own. That was the beginning of a courtship that lasted
one whole morning.

I went downstairs to my car to get the half-a-quarter of
cocaine while she waited at the bar. When I got back the
joint was thick with people crushed together choking off the
breath of the lone red bulb high up in the ceiling. I swam
through the sea of people and smoke until I found her leaning against the bar. I pulled her into the bathroom and
pressed the aluminum foil into her hand. We sat down, her
on the toilet seat, me on the edge of the tub close to her.

140

She passed me the blow. Everything she did was making me feel dry inside. This broad was getting to me!

I started rapping about myself, making sure to mention that I'd been to college and had worked for CBS both on and off the tube. I wanted her to know that I thought I was class enough for her—a different type hustler, one who had skated on white ice and found it too thin. There wasn't any sense in telling her I was married and had two kids. Shit, me and Ava were only lying under the same roof. Our marriage was just waiting for the undertaker! Why should I take a chance on sinking the ship before it sailed?

Pepper never took her eyes off my face as I talked. When I'd finished and asked her to leave with me, she reached for my hand.

It was near five when we left, hurrying down a dirty, piss-smelling flight of stairs. I felt like I was me Tarzan, her Jane! We made the rounds of one after-hours joint after another. I was showing her off in the high-class places that my cop man had taken me to, down in the 80s. Places with closed-circuit television monitoring the doors. The places were owned by the Mafia, and every dude got patted down before he got in, except the bulldog-looking Wops who came to pick up the cash. The ladies had only to open their bags. Pepper held onto my arm, squeezing it tightly, making me feel like she was proud of me, like she belonged to me and was glad of it! She liked excitement and excitement went with her. As we sat sniffing coke and sipping champagne at a table close to a marble indoor pool, she softly whispered her story to me. Her name was Pepper, she was twenty-two, married, she had three kids, and she, her mother, and her husband, who was not supporting her or the kids, all hustled numbers.

I got home at 10 o'clock the next morning, dropped on the sofa, and thought of the shameless affection she gave me, in public as well as when we'd been alone in the hotel making love. The respect she made me feel when the big-time Whitey gangsters offered her a drink or a blow when

141

we were at those heavyweight clubs. "That's quite all right, thank you, my man doesn't allow me to do that and I think he's right." Ladylike all the way. She never forgot to smile. She carried herself like a princess until she wrapped around me in bed. She was a tonic. I had asked her just before we left the hotel room: "Baby, what do you want to do about us?"

She sat back on the bed and looked through my eyes, and what she said went down into the depths of my suffering soul.

"If you want me, I'm yours. But don't ever leave me."

The memory dissolved as Ava shuffled into the living room and looked down at me for a moment with colorless eyes.

"I'm moving upstate Monday. I'm taking the kids with me."

I got up and walked over to the window and peeked between dirt-crusted blinds.

The undertaker was knocking at the door.

* * *

"Hey, man, how are you?"

It was Jimmy Watson on the phone, a welcome voice in my difficult day. I was only recently installed as News Director of WCBS-TV, and the stress was heavy.

I had not seen him since he had left CBS. I had failed then to convince him he should stay. I did not know what he was doing now. I had heard that someone had seen him at the Muhammad Ali fight dressed in a fur coat and glittering with jewels. Hmmmmm.

"Yeah, Jimmy, I'm the News Director now. We're all changing. What are you up to?"

"Oh this and that. Say, Mike, I may have a story for you, a drug story. Think you'd be interested?"

"Yeah, I'm interested. Also like to see you."

"Why don't I come by this afternoon and pick you up?"

"Okay. Make it around 3."

142

There was no mistaking the car parked on 57th Street. It was the same length as the black Cadillacs that glided out of the CBS garage adjoining Black Rock on 52d Street, bearing division presidents to their homes in Connecticut each evening, parading up the East River Drive. But Jimmy's car was dark gold, and his black face with the bold, slightly hooded eyes peered at me through the tinted window, his cap swooping over his left ear—alert like a country cat feeling a change in the wind. Jimmy was obviously doing well. The rumors I had heard must be true. Jimmy was a hustler and the elaborate car was his office.

"Mike! How are yuh?" He was friendly and equal now, no longer the subtle deference of the apprentice and the boss.

Later, inside a bar on Third Avenue, sitting by the window, Jimmy picked out from the constant clutter of cars moving up the avenue those of the hustlers heading uptown toward Harlem and the Bronx to look after business—white Eldorados with whitewall tires and extra chrome, Lincolns with customized tire wells jutting like upthrust second fingers from the trunk, metallic sky-blue Cadillacs, all of them with little expensive ornaments—an early evening promenade of numbers writers, dope dealers, and super pimps.

Jimmy talked about money.

"Two, three, four thousand a day, man. A DAY. ALL I want. I've done moved my wife and kids out of the city, man. Got them a house in the country where they can breathe." He showed me what he had in his pocket, a thick wad of bills, maybe a thousand dollars right there in his hip pocket.

As the second drink took hold, the stories flowed: the hustler parties where the girls would lick off the cocaine he had sprinkled on the head of his cock; the motel room with the mirrors on the ceiling over the bed where he could watch the thrashing bodies of the five women who enveloped him; the pimps and the pimps' women who would be available to love or beat, depending on the mood; and

143

the flamboyant trips to Jamaica, where a black hustler from New York could splash his money around with the whites untroubled.

Money, sex, and travel—the *Playboy* fantasy. Jimmy was coming on, trying to convince me he was living it. And then, switching abruptly to another level: how he wanted me and him to do something together, to expose the drug traffic, to write something about the racket. Painstaking analysis of his business to convince me he hated those who sold smack to kids. He was coming at me on a variety of levels in that bar on Third Avenue, playing on what he imagined were my fantasies and biases, searching for my approval.

Then later, late in the night, sitting on the right side of the front seat, Pepper sitting between us, all of us sniffing cocaine—my first time—on the way through the black, stenching streets of the South Bronx to pick up a woman for me. I was being treated to a night on hustler town. And while we waited in his car for her to come I asked him about the tension and danger that all night I had sensed around us, in the hooded looks from the sidewalk idlers as we cruised by, in the grunted conversations with people who detached themselves from the clusters when we stopped, in and out of bars gaseous with menace, making deals. He turned to me and said yes, there were dangers, but:

"I feel like a man now, Mike. Do you unnerstan'? I feel like a man."

She joined us then, a beautiful, dusky girl of about twenty. I got in the back seat with her. She looked out the window, said a few words to Pepper, occasionally sent a brief, strained smile in my direction, then sat like a stone. Later in a bar, I asked Jimmy about the girl.

"The girl is nice, Jimmy, but I don't know, man. Nothing is happening between us, you know what I mean. She doesn't react one way or another. She's like dead."

Jimmy's head was full of coke now, and he and his woman were cuddling. Impatience edged his voice.

144

"Do what you want with her, man. Tell her what you want. She's yours."

I looked at her, sitting silent there, and I gazed around the bar catching flickers of bloodshot dark eyes returning to their frontward looking gaze as my eyes passed over them and knew they would be back on me when I turned again to my table—the only white man in an environment so strange that I had difficulty believing in its existence, having no connections there to anyone, not the female beside me who was said to be mine, not to Jimmy, not to anyone in the bar, not even to the neighborhood, although it was part of the city in which I lived. Disembodied. So I told the girl I thought she was just fine, but I was tired, and I asked Jimmy to drop me off at a safe corner where I hailed a cab and returned to Manhattan and home, leaving Jimmy's quizzical look behind. Home, rich in texture and warm in flannel familiarity. It was good to get home.

* * *

Stan said his nerves were bad. He had been seeing too many narcos around lately.

"Let's get outta the country for a while, man!"

I thought he was jiving.

"Where?" I asked.

"You pick it. Somewhere warm, but not Puerto Rico. Stinks down there."

A TV commercial jumped into my mind—"I just love Jamaica!"

"How 'bout Jamaica?"

"That's good," he said through his perfectly manicured teeth. "That's boss. Make the reservations." He started to leave. "I'll be back. Gotta pick up some scratch."

Pepper had overheard the whole conversation, and she got busy packing. We weren't going without her.

In a few hours we sped off to Kennedy Airport in a white and gold Fleetwood.

I had never flown first class before. It had seemed stupid to pay about a hundred dollars more for a free drink. You could bring your own and drink it in the bathroom; the plane got everybody there at the same time. But first class turned out to be more than a free drink. You were treated first class—those superfine stewardesses grinned and fussed over us like we were precious VIPs!

We were all clean and diamonded down. Stan had $11,000 worth of stones set in platinum wrapped around his left middle finger. I had $15,000 worth of carats on mine, and Pepper was sparkling too—ears, neck, and four fingers.

The other first-class folks—all white—were wondering with their eyes: Who in the hell could these niggers be, looking so fine and dandy? They smiled and made small talk about the weather, probing for an opening to get more personal. I didn't like talking to white folks, period. Stan didn't dig rapping to white men. So Pepper wound up talking to the white dudes, Stan jawing and acting smooth with the stewardesses, and me wishing they would all shut up. Finally, the little blonde, pinched-nose stewardess asked me were we entertainers? That was the question everyone had been waiting for! Everybody got real quiet.

"We're in the oil business," I told her, "and rich as shit!"

She laughed nervously and hurried away. Whether she and the rest of the white folks believed my big lie, I don't know. But they sure stopped being so nosy.

Jamaica was just like the man on TV said it was—clear and colorful, ripe and juicy as a piece of fruit, too warm for my heavy New York clothes.

We picked a hotel in Montego Bay from one of the many posters plastered all over the Jamaican Information Center. It was a slick-looking joint, off-white trimmed in gold and rosewood, that crawled out past a sifted beach into the Caribbean. Stan paid the cab driver and we registered. A lazy bellboy led us down a red-carpeted hallway to our rooms —a wooden double bed, two chests of drawers and two straw

146

chairs crouched under a ceiling so long a giant must have stepped on it. On the far side, away from the bed, a double sliding glass door opened onto a cement terrace so close to the sea the spray made it shine like marble. I tipped the bell-boy, showered, and changed clothes—summer stuff, out of Leighton's and Phil Kronfeld's, clothes of matching colors, flowing together. Rich colors, like the country, like the way I felt!

We spent our first night out up in the hills buying reefer, smoking reefer, buying more reefer, and smoking more reefer, joints a foot long and an inch wide. Our guide was our cab driver, Joe. He took us from place to place, making contacts for us. I guess he had done this many times before, because all the pot sellers greeted him like a welfare check. We spent about ten dollars for a half-pound, and the tall, soot-black Jamaican who sold it to us trembled with joy as he took the cash and folded it into his pocket.

As we were about to take off, he stopped us and motioned to Joe. The tall Jamaican had dug a good thing. The two of them walked over to a low-hanging tree, said a few words, and came back to us.

"How wouldja like to go pull on de pipe?" his thick black lips slapping the words at us.

"How much it gonna cost?" By now I had started to dig where these Jamaicans were coming from—they didn't take any money from you, they just kept you giving it to them.

"Naaaatttt muuuuch."

He was a hustler all right. We was on his territory, and he knew he had what we wanted. Yeah, me and him had a lot in common. But not in color. He was the blackest dude I'd ever seen in my life.

We left our driver and followed the tall Jamaican in his ragged, grimy shorts down under some deserted wharves, thick with grass, bushes, and weeds. A group of four men stood around a small fire.

Shit, I thought, maybe these dudes is gonna take us off.

147

I pulled Stan over to me and ran down what I had in my mind. It wasn't cool to say nothing to Pepper, because she might panic and start acting nervous.

Stan shook his head. "Naw, man, these people ain't like that. Come on!" He laughed and strode on ahead toward the firelit circle of men.

When we reached the group, they were all smiling, looking real friendly, like it was meal time and dinner had just arrived.

The dude who brought us here, Roy, introduced us as "big pot smokers from New York City in the States" and said he'd invited us to "pull on the pipe." All eight eyes bulged in concert, and the four ragged Jamaicans we'd just met grunted and gestured in disbelief.

A jet-black, prune-skinned, mostly toothless dude looked at me. "Man, have you ev-vah pooled de pipe befo'?"

"Naw man, but I smoked two of them foot-long reefers yuh man Roy gave me and I ain't high yet. So if it's the same shit it ain't gonna have no better effect outa a pipe."

He backed off, still grinning through holes in his rotted mouth, bent down and opened what looked like a large, green laundry bag.

I glanced at Stan. He had his eyes dead on the dude with the bag. Pepper was gripping my arm tightly, nervous with excitement. Maybe she had noticed the three-foot-long machetes each of those guys had tied to his side.

The pipe Prune Skin pulled out of that bag was the size of a bass saxophone and looked twice as heavy. It was a wooden carved figure of a man in a swan dive, head drawn back, mouth wide open, legs arched up and back with feet close together.

Stan let out a loud "Daaaaaammmmmmm!" when he saw it.

I felt Pepper's grip tighten. "Oooooooh, shit," she whispered.

Man, I thought, how much does that thing hold? I know they ain't going to fill it!

Another dude, named Twelve Fingers because he had that

148

many fingers and toes, broke out the reefer, spoke some prayerful shit over it, then handed it to Prune Skin, who began packing it in the mouth of the carved figure, packing it tightly with short jabs of his fist. Another man held the pipe around the legs and by the feet. There were holes in both big toes to draw in the smoke.

The statue's dick stood erect and was made of glass. It was filled with rum, so Roy said, through which the reefer smoke would pass on the way to your lungs.

A light-skinned, red-haired dude named Red took a burning piece of wood from the fire and held it to the mouth while Prune Face sucked on the toes to get it started. Then they began passing the pipe from man to man, not inhaling, just sucking on it easy, blowing the smoke out, getting it going real good!

Then Twelve Fingers took hold of the pipe and with another dude standing behind him started puffing hard and fast. All of a sudden the other four dudes, Roy included, shouted: "Hit it, mon!" and Twelve Fingers sucked in with all his might while the dude behind him reached over and pulled a plug which acted as a damper from between the buttocks of the diving figure. A billow of smoke shot up and engulfed us all, and Twelve Fingers' corner man held him tightly around the waist to keep him from falling. Prune Skin grabbed the pipe as it began to fall from Twelve Fingers' grasp.

Everyone stood staring at Twelve Fingers, who had gone limp, eyelids shut. In a few seconds he opened his eyes, and the Jamaicans roared with laughter.

It was Red's turn. Prune Skin passed him the pipe and took up the corner man's position behind him. Red did his thing—puffing hard then rising up on his toes and drawing deep when the chorus shouted "Hit it, mon!" trying to outdo Twelve Fingers' performance. He didn't pass out, but his face turned dark brown and his eyes flooded as he struggled to hold the smoke down in his chest. Prune Face followed Red on the pipe, and then a long, snake-looking dude called

Slim who'd kept Twelve Fingers from falling took his turn.

By this time, the area under the wharf was thick with smoke. All four of them dudes were high, man, wiped out, hollering, stomping around. Red was so twisted he almost fell into the fire. In the midst of the noise and the funning, Prune Skin screamed at me:

"Doo yoo waaaant to pool on de pipe now, mon? Doo yoo tink yoo con stand eet?" His body was bent forward almost in two, shaking with laughter, his rusty eyes squinting, waiting for me to answer, the fire casting his satanic shadow against the back wall.

"Man," I told him, "ain't no way in the world I'm gonna fuck with that thing!"

He howled and slapped his thigh hard. That dried-up, bony motherfucker looked so funny hopping around, messed up in the head, laughing his ass off, I bust out hee-hawing myself. Then I dug that everybody was laughing and had been splitting their sides all the while—the Jamaicans, Pepper, and Stan. I had been so tensed up I hadn't realized everyone, including me, was stoned. Pepper had her back up against an old beam, head leaning back to one side, knees sagging, tears streaming down her cheeks, cracking up. Stan had sat down on an old drum, his long legs forcing his knees up to his face, hands gripping his ankles, coughing with laughter. We were all laughing at one another and for the good feeling you get from laughing. We'd let our hair down and the Jamaicans dug it. We could have fun now. We had money, but none of us was gonna pull on that pipe. They could pull on de pipe but didn't have no money. That made us even. Didn't make no difference who had what, we was all high!

❁ ❁ ❁

Joe, our cab driver, told us that the Peacock Club was the top spot in Montego Bay. "All de big entertainers on the island play dere."

We jumped double clean into semiformal evening wear and hit the joint; ordered drinks and got set to enjoy the big show the barker at the entrance said would be going on in three minutes.

On stage a Jamaican marimba band had the atmosphere throbbing, thumping, and jumping. A conga drum rolled, and out leaped four dancers in green diapers—a guy and a girl from each wing. They did their number, yelling loud and jumping around, feet kicking, arms thrashing the air like wild people. Then the pace slowed and the dancers brought out two long, thick bamboo poles. One couple, a man at one end, a girl at the other, knelt down, picked up the poles and began slapping them together low to the floor in time with the music, while the other couple hopped in and out between the slapping poles, lifting their legs just before the poles clacked together. They really put on a show!

The short, black, big-headed master of ceremonies with a sticky Jamaican accent warned that if those poles slammed against an ankle, the ankle would crack wide open. That thought struck him funny and he leaned back and howled. When he stopped hee-hawing, he asked for volunteers from the audience.

His eyes lit on Pepper and he motioned for her to come up and try.

"Eh, man," I hollered to him, "she gets *paid* to entertain, an' I just paid to have *you* entertain her!"

He flashed a gold, toothy grin, but I knew he didn't like it.

He pointed to some Whiteys waving their arms for his attention and at the same time shot me an evil eye. Them white folks were so uncoordinated they would have been crippled for life if it weren't for the skill of the black folks controlling the slapping poles. One stiff-jointed old white broad jumped so high, hard, and fast her earrings fell off. When she'd finished and accepted her applause the big-headed master of ceremonies picked them up for her.

"Lay-dee, you dropped dese. Let me see, what are dey?

151

Ooooooo, liddle monkeys. Dey look jees lak me—ooooooo-oohhh, ha ha." Hahahahahaha!

Man, I couldn't believe my ears! I turned to Stan and Pepper. They stared back as amazed as I was. The black sonof-abitch couldn't leave off with that. His mouth got even shittier.

"All black pee-pole look lak mon-keeeys. White pee-pole look good and pretty, lak angels—aaaaaaaaaaahahahahahaha."

I could have put my foot in his ass. The three of us rose to leave at the same time. Stan was so fucking mad he'd a turned red if he'd been lighter.

"You people are a hundred years behind times," he screamed and strutted out slinging his arms, me and Pepper close at his heels.

The next few days were spent playing in the ocean and toasting on the beach. We ignored the "No Phonographs or Radios on the Beach" signs. Shit, we had to play some soul on that new portable record player Stan had just bought. When the hotel's law enforcer came to investigate, I did just what I'd do in New York—flipped him a bribe. He took it, turned around, and marched back across the sand—ears, eyes and mouth closed!

We liked the clear, clean, pretty water, the sun-bleached sand, the fancy hotel, and the slavish service. We did not like the high wire fence dividing the beach, separating the choicest, most beautiful side for the hotel's paying guests from the shitty side, jagged with coral reefs and old logs, where the native blacks did their swimming and sunning.

"Damn, Stan, white man fuck black folks around wher-ever he go!"

We were lying in the sand under a large white umbrella listening to Aretha Franklin, with Pepper singing along in the background, giving Aretha some help, watching the Jamaicans on the other side of the fence making body move-ments in time to the music. Now and then one of them would call over to us asking who was singing and whether the singer was a "black brudder" or "black seester."

152

"Man, Whitey fuck anybody around that ain't got no money. Them dudes on the other side of the fence could be on this side if they had the cash." Stan looked at me and laughed. "Ain't it good to have cash!"

It damn sure was!

11 Free time!

The thought struck me one afternoon sitting in a chair in my bedroom, the afternoon sun brightening the page of *The Greening of America* on my lap. I had never had free time since leaving college. Outside of one- and two-week vacations, I had always been working.

Now, after fifteen years, I had time without demands, time to think, to read, to assess, nothing to do but cash the CBS paycheck which kept coming in regularly every two weeks. I was still on the payroll, but I had rejected the one offer the company had made me, so I was without assignment but still being paid, and the company was not rushing me. I knew I would resign eventually, but in the meantime I needed that cash. It bought me time in which to figure out what to do next.

I did not have any idea of what I would do. There wasn't a job I could think of that interested me. I felt nonfunctional, with a wife and four kids to support, adrift and anxious, stripped of my familiar structure of job, position, place in society.

I felt the self-induced pressure upon me to rush out and

get another task, one in which I would wrestle and strive and create a great achievement. Show those bastards!

But I also knew that these moments of free time were a precious gift, a gift that could be used for a renewal of my exhausted and unhappy spirit. So I restrained the urge to rush back into the fray. No, I would not go back. I would move on somewhere else. But where was that?

One thing had been tugging at me for the past few years —the cultural revolution of the late '60s. I admired every bit of it, especially its freedom. The rebellious young captured my attention, as they did everyone's in the media. All my secret hangups were being paraded by them right out there where everyone could see, and it was said to be okay—do your own thing; it's all right with us. None of that guilt, that constant measuring of motivation, the evaluation of people, that bleak morality so hypocritical in its practices and joyless in its effect.

In the face of that new and theatrical freedom, I felt that a great part of my life had consisted of a process in which I had been polished, licked, kissed, brushed, cleaned, pushed, beaten, threatened, and frightened by the ruling tribe preparing its young to become the next generation of controllers to consolidate the gains, protect the retiring, and turn over intact to the following generation of the white tribe the reins of power. I had learned about duty, responsibility, honor, achievement, and I had learned to speak without telling, feel without displaying, take without giving. But I had never learned to smile without happiness, as so many of my peers had.

Now, sitting there in the overstuffed chair in the afternoon sun, restoring myself, I decided that the time had come to have more of life; that this expansion would not be presented to me by a new job, by a new location, by another person or group of persons. Its achievement depended solely on myself. I had to find my own way.

I had discovered drugs a few years before and had acquired a taste. Marijuana was delightful, adding soft dimensions to my life and a texture to my social relationships that I had never before experienced. I drank less liquor, and that felt good. LSD astonished me.

In my quiet time, I decided that what I needed most was to delve within myself and discover the feelings I sensed straining within but which I could not quite release. I wanted those feelings to instruct me as to what I should do with myself and how I should look upon the experiences I had recently undergone. I chose LSD for the trip within and read all the literature before I began.

* * *

One afternoon, in Barbara's basement apartment, we both dropped acid with the mutual understanding that we would create an environment for each other's self-explorations. We would not impose our presence on each other, but we each would lend the other as much security as the other desired.

I examined the workings of my own mind, while Barbara sat at the foot of the bed into her own journey. We had been lovers for a few years, and I felt comfortable with her. My mind was millions of minuscule red and green cells flashing and blinking brilliantly in a symmetrical pattern, very precise but too complex to be comprehended. It was a landscape of color and electric activity stretching on infinitely, the vastest computer circuit imaginable, flashing and whirring away. I was watching the cells of my mind do their precise dance of life energy. It was stunningly beautiful.

I made the cells whir faster to figure out how someone's personality operates in causing that person to act. Barbara was staring into the other room, her profile visible. I began tracing one of her familiar actions to its beginning to her bubbling cells. My brain raced, filling my head with pressure. Sensing the energy crossing the space between us, Barbara turned to me. I felt an engulfing unity well up between us. The bone that covered her forehead appeared to dissolve, as

156

did mine, and fibers grew between our heads, linking us, bringing us together not as a man and a woman who pleassured each other but as humans linked as one in their humanity. I felt the unity of all humans and understood then the relentless pursuit of people seeking other people to talk to them, hug them, kiss them, penetrate or be penetrated by them, spill out to them their innermost yearnings—why they clustered together in cities, parties, bars, beds. Yes, we all nourish each other and feed off each other, like a circle. All those exhortations to love one another that I never quite understood. Now I understood, and I knew I was undergoing one of the most magnificent and revelatory experiences of my life.

"My God. God. This is fantastic!" I blurted it out. I was unable to articulate it further because it was so vast that it would have taken a thousand words to communicate it and I did not want to stop the experience to assemble the words. I wanted to flow on, feel more, learn more.

Before me now was the world and all of its people, a great mass of humanity undulating on the globe—spaceship earth —and with my mind functioning as a zoom lens I located myself in the midst of all of those people, a speck in the midst of the crowd, an element in the whole. It was perspective in reverse of my usual one—I was not an individual on a high bluff looking down at the rest of the world, now I was only a part within the whole. So why should I be trying to control the world as though I had such power, such uniqueness? I sensed then how much wiser it would be to flow, instead of struggling and battering. The rock that had been lodged in the stream bed causing eddies to whirl in disturbance behind it dislodged at that moment and began to tumble along in the current. It was soothing.

And now the disembodied abstract observer that was my mind entered the cosmos itself, seeing the world and its billions as itself only one element in a larger, infinite galaxy, and there was I, still visible to the zoom lens, a speck within

157

this vastness, insignificant but yet me. I felt like waving to myself down there among it all.

Now I arrived at the very root of myself, and I got up from the bed, strode through the living room into the bathroom, looked up at my harried face in the mirror, and saw within it all the pain and pleasure of my life. At that moment I was overwhelmed with the conviction that I could now choose: life or death. It was the first time I had so directly faced such a choice. It would need no physical act on my part, merely a decision. If I chose to live, I would continue my trip in Barbara's apartment. If I chose death, I would keel over right then, dead of some thoroughly natural cause, heart failure or something.

Irish sentiment overcame me then. I thought of my wife and children, all weeping over my death. I almost swooned with the love I felt for them. And I thought of the difficulty for Barbara if I were to die there—MARRIED MAN SUC-CUMBS IN GIRLFRIEND'S APARTMENT!—and then it all became too much for me. I freaked. I was frightened by the edge at which I stood.

Down. Down. Enough lessons for today, and with a flexing of self-control I pulled myself away from that level to more familiar ground.

The memory of that new vision of freedom remained with me after the experience was over. I had learned that the richer life I wanted was not one I could design, manipulate, cause to happen. It would happen to me only to the degree that I opened myself to its possibilities and let them happen to me. I would swim along with the current in which I had been placed, using the best strokes I knew.

❉   ❉   ❉

Over the years, my wife and I had enough resilience in our marriage to adjust to the personal changes we encouraged in each other. We both had a dread of that state of near-

158

death which marriage produced in most of our former friends. But she was pained deeply when, after nine years of marriage, I had my first affair, when I fell in love and blurted it all out to her in a paroxysm of guilt and shame.

I never returned to the monogamous state after that. It seemed too narrow, too austere, even though I knew I was causing Kathie pain. Through the wrenches and the angers, we eventually arrived at a state of acceptance of each other's sexual freedom, attempting mightily to control our jealousy, our urge to possess each other exclusively. The efforts we made on each other's behalf drew us closer than we had ever been.

But it became an increasing strain for her, because my changes seemed to be galloping along; freedom was a constantly expanding concept. She yearned for tranquility. Now I was heading out again, pushing out the barriers once more. I could feel the notion developing that we had lived together so long and in so rigid and formal a structure that radical change was impossible.

At some point it seemed to occur to us simultaneously that we would have to live apart if we were to stop the growth of the insidious idea that she was blocking my path and I hers. Neither of us wanted the resentment that was building.

She was sitting on the sofa in the living room. I was on a chair beside her. We had drinks and began to talk, as we did each evening we were together, long talks exploring our relationship, our feelings toward each other. I told her of my new thoughts, my new experiences, an interesting woman I had met. She interrupted me:

"It's all over, isn't it?"

I was startled and frightened. She had forced the issue, courageously, directly. It was not time for bullshit.

I looked into her green eyes, her soft face more familiar to me than my own. The pain ached.

"I guess I better move out."

I joined her on the sofa then. We held hands and cried together for the rest of the evening.

*   *   *

Shortly before I moved to a three-room apartment on Riverside Drive, I was approached by someone who had worked for me at WCBS-TV. He was about to become General Manager of WRVR, an FM radio station. He wanted to make the station all news, radical in its approach to journalism. He wanted me to help him design the broadcasts, then function as the host of the station's major news show, doing exactly what I felt like doing. I accepted the job.

*   *   *

"In many ways, you and I grew up together, and, in other ways, we grew apart. What I like in these particular circumstances is that we did grow apart together. I sense that the apart had to grow bigger, but for all the world I could not say why."—letter from my ex-wife.

160

12   I'd been asleep on the convertible sofa we kept in the office when the click of the turning lock woke me. I raised myself up and watched as they entered. "Boss."

I was struck by the word, pleased but uncomfortable, like when I was first called mister.

Karl and Jhonny, two of the cruelest, most sadistic dudes I'd ever met, stepped through the office door they had just unlocked. They were preceded by Fang and Killer, two giant Dobermans trained to attack.

"Boss, that jive motherfucker wasn't home!" Jhonny said.

He was in his early thirties, average height, brown-complexioned, thick mustache. Good looking. Karl was thirty-six, near the same height, lighter-complexioned, clean-shaven face and head. You'd say he was good looking too. Both carried pot bellies, and when teased about their stomachs they'd claim that the girls like a big-gut nigger, said fat bellies gave the ho's something to play on. A "chippie's playground" they said.

"Me and Karl sat parked out there all night waiting fo' his ass, but he never showed."

161

Jhonny and his brother were feared sons a bitches who would shoot, cut, stab, or bludgeon a dude in a minute. The scars on their bodies—gunshot and knife wounds—showed they hadn't always been on the giving end of pain. Whenever we were alone with some fine young hustling bitches, Karl and Jhonny always made sure that they pulled off something, shirt or pants, to expose a closed up bullet hole or a stitched up knife rip. The young ho's would be impressed —these dudes is for real! And they would allow us to do anything we wanted to with their bodies. We would have each bitch all together—a dick in every hole, ass, cunt, and mouth, or we'd each take one, one at a time. Either way, they got down, all the way down. Group sex, all of us coked up and freaking off. It ain't shit! Better alone with one woman you dig than with ten you don't. But that was sport, fun, what was happennnnnnnning!

"How you know he wasn't in his house?" I was looking up at them, asking for an explanation as they stood over me. The dogs moved around, noses to the floor, sniffing in all the corners of the two-and-a-half-room apartment.

"We looked! His wife answered the door, said he wasn't home, but we pushed past her and checked out the pad. Fang and Killer made sure she didn't start no shit."

I sat up, kicking the covers off my naked ass. "Pass me my pants. . . . Get them fucking dogs outa the damn garbage!"

Karl took my pants from the back of the chair and passed them to me, bellowing to the dogs at the same time: "Over here!"

Fang and Killer leaped to his side.

"In the corner," he bellowed again, pointing the direction with his finger. At once they moved to the corner by the window, and sat there panting, tongues dripping saliva.

I was moving up in the dope world and had hired Jhonny and Karl as lieutenants. They took care of the distribution and collection. And I mean took care! A dude either paid for the drugs I gave him on consignment or he paid the doctor. In some cases, his family paid the undertaker—Jhonny

162

and Karl saw to that! They cost me $400 a week apiece. I was a generous boss, often giving them a small package of heroin worth maybe two, three hundred on the street.

The dogs were a specialty. Whenever Jhonny and Karl spotted a dude who owed and who'd been ducking, they'd approach him. If he ran, the dogs would be turned loose. "Get 'em." A motherfucker either stopped dead and stood still or got half his ass ate up.

Jhonny and Karl did fucked up things with those dogs, like making dudes—usually guys who'd crossed them—suck the dogs' dicks, or have the dogs fuck some poor bastard in his asshole, all at gun point. I didn't like or trust them dogs nor their masters. When would they turn on me?

"What else did Dopey's wife have to say?" I pulled out a baggie filled with cocaine and dropped it on the coffee table. Jhonny opened it, grinning, and greedily filled his matchbook quill.

"Sniffffftt . . . whew. . . . She said he went to visit his mother in Philly. She 'bout to die or somethin'."

The wall mirror hanging by the closet said today was not red-leather day as I stood in front of it. I put the red leather shirt back on its hanger and stepped back from the closet, forgetting about something to wear and reaching for the blow.

"Why his momma gotta git sick jus' when he owe me 15 gran'?" I cracked. "That nigger jus' stallin'." I took two quick blows, feeling the cocaine rush through my body. Uuuuuuuuh!

I dropped back down on the sofa, thinking about that money. That was what the game was all about, what any professional game is all about. Money. I'd always wanted some money, $220, $300 a week—real good job money. You know, 10 to 15 grand a year working money. I knew one day I'd be making that kind of cash. I never thought about more than 15–20 grand a year, except for wishful thinking like that I could be Captain Marvel—SHAZAM!—or Henry Aldrich and live on Elm Street. To me 15–20 grand didn't seem spectacular, not when you read the help wanted section of the *Times*. But now I knew that the only help I'd

163

get outa that section was when I wiped my ass with it. Now I looked to see that much cash for myself every three months. Hell, I knew niggers that put that much cocaine up their noses in less than twelve months. Niggers who dealt in dope, in heroin!

But now I was stretched way out. I'd never let any one dude owe me that much cash before. If I didn't collect, word would get around. Other niggers might get ideas about not paying. I took a deep breath, leaned back on the sofa and scratched my balls. I had to tell Jhonny and Karl what was happening; get them ready for action.

"I see why they call this nigger Dopey. He got to be a fool. Shit, he give up $2,500 on a seventeen-five grand package and tell me some jive 'bout he'll straighten it out with Stan."

Karl laid his matchbook quill on the table, his eyes bulging wide. "He gonna do what? He tol' you that he gone straighten the bill out with Stan? That motherfucker got to be going out of his mind!"

Karl didn't like it—a worker telling his boss that he would straighten out business with somebody else. That was not the way it was done. That was disrespecting the boss. And when the boss was disrespected, Karl and Jhonny were disrespected. He couldn't get away with that.

"Well, what you want us to do now?" Jhonny asked.

"Nothing 'till I talk to his wife. With all the money she been stealing she got to have some stashed away. All I want is my money. I think she'll understand. If she don't, well, we'll see."

I got up then and started to finish dressing. I had not been upstairs all night, and Pepper was probably smoking her ass off about now. I found an old olive drab wool sweater and a pair of bell bottoms from my City College days and began slipping them on.

"Going home now, huh?"

"You goddamn right." I slipped on my sneakers using my finger as a shoe horn. "Pepper came down last night and

164

rang the doorbell not long after a couple of them young ho's got here. I didn't answer; don't know if she knew they was here or not."

"Yo' ass in trouble, my man."

Jhonny looked at Karl and both started grinning in that sly-ass way.

"How much merchandise we got left?"

"Thirteen hunnert halves!" Jhonny shot it to me fast. He ran the cutting table, he's supposed to know. "Joe stashed 'em over Anne's house."

That's the way it was done—my way. And my way meant cut and move, cut and move. Never keep it where you cut it, and keep a guy with it at all times.

"Anne got a phone?"

"Yeah. Joe gave it to me in case we wanted him early," Karl answered.

"Then call his ass up and tell him to come on over to the office. Then you call Dopey's wife and tell her I wanna see her!"

I left the ground-floor office, climbing stairs heading for the fifth floor where Pepper and me lived.

"One bell less to answer, one less egg to fryyyyy." It was Nancy Wilson's voice sprinkling down from the fifth floor. Yeah, Pepper was *hot*, man, warning me with Nancy's song that she was about to explode.

I hesitated at the fifth floor, trying to think of a lie. Then I got mad. What lie did I have to make up? Shit, I didn't owe her no excuse. I was taking care of her ass, spending *my* cash on her, helping her with her kids, taking her out of the country—Jamaica, Haiti, Puerto Rico. Shit! She was living like a movie star compared to how she'd lived before. FUCK HER! ! ! I rang the buzzer.

I heard her coming to the door, stopping first to turn the music down. Shit, I took her out of the ghetto, man. She had it made—her man was the BOSS.

"Who?" she called through the door in her sing-song, little-girl voice.

165

"Me, baby."

"Where's yo' keys?"

"Never mind that shit, open the fuckin' door!"

The door opened as I spoke.

What a sight. A fine motherfucker standing in the doorway in leotards with a kitchen apron around her small waist, hair falling down around her shoulders, eyes flashing, holding a dish towel in her hand.

"Hi ya, woman." I leaned to kiss her. "Gimme some."

"Didn't you get some where you was at?" She turned her back and started for the kitchen. That's when I noticed the smell. Whatever she was cooking in there, she was doing it good. The woman was mean on a pot, and I do mean MEAN!

"Wait a minute, motherfucker," I yelled. "Come 'ere an' gimme mine!" She was walking away from me, shaking her little ass. I lunged, grabbing her shoulders and snatching the dish towel from her hand, throwing it to the floor as I turned her toward me and pressed her close. She didn't pull back.

"Come 'ere motherfucker," I whispered.

"Didn't you get enough from the bitches you was with all night?"

I shut her mouth with mine, found her tongue, sucked on it.

"Uuuuuuuuuummmmmmmmmmmmmuuuuuuuuuuhhhhhhhh," we moaned as I slid both arms around her, squeezing her ass in my hands.

◊　◊　◊

Pepper was sleeping now, naked, twisted on her stomach, her right knee stepping up, climbing to her breast. Her hair, a black river, rushed down the white pillow case, fell off at her shoulders, made a curving sweep along her brown vel-vet back and disappeared at the base of her spine. She slept with her lips slightly open, mouth filled with little pearls that looked as though they would fall out if you touched

166

her head. Yeah! Sure she'd had a ball in Jamaica and a ball when she got back, all tan and fly. She had bounced around to all the hustling bars, showing off her pictures, her new ring, modeling her tan like a commercial until it wore off. The trip had boosted her status to queen and she didn't let the other bitches or my billfold forget it! That was all right: I was her king!

But that was enough of reminiscences. It was now late afternoon, and there were things that needed doing. I jumped out of bed, showered quickly, then stamped back into the bedroom to get dressed.

The phone rang sharply, waking Pepper as I was slipping a knitted red wool, vee-necked sweater over my head. I snatched up the receiver. It was Karl.

"Hey, boss," his voice rasped from too much cocaine. "You coming down? We got Dopey here."

"Who went got him?"

"Nobody. He come by himself!"

"He bring the money?" My tone was flat.

"Naw! But he say he want to talk to you!"

My mouth dripped blood!

"That motherfucker— I'll be right there!" I slammed the receiver down and sat on the edge of the bed. Pepper rolled over and gripped my thigh.

"What's the matter, honey?"

"I ain't sure!" the words bit at her. "But I know one stupid sonofabitch who better tell me!"

Fear crossed her brow as I stood up and strode over to the other side of the bed. I jerked open the polished dresser and pulled out the blue steel Smith & Wesson .357 magnum. I broke it open and counted five dum-dum slugs in the cylinder, then tucked it in my waistband and pulled the bulky red sweater into place.

Pepper was watching every move I made. She called me as I started out the door:

"Honey, I'm going down to Mama's. . . . I'll fix dinner there."

"Okay, baby."

I took my time loping down the stairs, holding my stomach. Couldn't have that big mag falling out of my pants. I didn't intend to shoot him, but something had to be done to this insane motherfucker. I needed that money, shit! I owed Andre 15 grand, and in the dope game there were no excuses for not paying that kind of money. Friendship was forgotten. Time was running out! If I didn't get that *cash* my whole organization would get shot to pieces—me first.

I stuck my key in the lock and pushed into the kitchen. It smelled greasy. Joe was hunched over the dinette table shoveling grits and eggs up to his face. I could see Karl in the living room, sitting in the rocker by the window, Fang and Killer at either side of his feet. Across from him, on the other side of the room, I spied Dopey, his face carved with fear, seated on the far end of the sofa holding his chin in his right hand. I couldn't see Jhonny.

Joe twisted his head, facing me. He was a Honduran, short and dark with a wide, fat nose hung like a teardrop in the center of his face. His shoulders were broad and sloped inward from too much time in jail bent over playing cards.

"What's happening?" he grunted, jaws working like pistons. He was the only one in the group I really trusted. My man!

"You tell me." I said it light, forcing a smile.

"Yo' ol' lady bust yo' ass?" It was Karl jugging with me from the next room. Karl always found time to joke around. I moved into the living room, feeling less tense now. Karl had set the tone—relaxed, doing it like a pro.

"Man, what is you, a reporter?" I jugged back at him, shooting a quick eye at Dopey who had dropped his hand from his chin when I entered the room. Jhonny was standing at the opposite end of the sofa leaning against the bureau, pointing a snub-nosed .38 at Dopey's head.

Dopey's expressions had all the troubles of the world. I kept on jugging with Karl.

168

"What paper you work for? The *Nosy Nigger News?*"
Karl laughed out loud at that one. He was enjoying the
game. The two giant Dobermans looked up at him, wagging
their stubby tails. Joe had just finished eating and came in
laughing to join the fun.

"Man," he snickered, "Karl told me Pepper gave you a
con-cush-shon!"

Karl grabbed at that: "She did! That's why the nigger was
upstairs so long. I started to call the ambulance!"

"We gonna need one. Maybe a hearse!" Jhonny spoke for
the first time, and there was no bullshit in his voice.

"We won't need either one. My dogs ain't et all day!"
Karl came in on cue. All eyes narrowed on Dopey. He sat
squirming like a black fish, eyes wide, mouth moving but not
making a sound.

Karl jumped to his feet suddenly and pointed at Dopey:
"Watch him!" he whispered. The two dogs sprang up bristling,
their mouths open showing those terrible two-inch fangs.

They stood frozen, daring Dopey to move so they could
eat him alive. Dopey got so still I thought he had fainted
with his eyes open.

As I watched him I felt power surge in me, feeding on
his fear. It was my move next. They were waiting. Jhonny
and Karl had started this deadly game, now it was up to me,
the boss, to say how I wanted it played. The power of life
and death had been laid on me too quickly: I didn't know
what to do. My lieutenants were cold-blooded killers, their
boss was not. But I damn sure couldn't let them know it. I
needed time to think. To shade my indecision, I slid my
hand under my sweater and pulled out my mag, eyes fixed
on Dopey, watching his grow wet. The punk was starting to
cry. His tears were giving me a reason to delay my move.

"Here, man," I was easing toward Jhonny, handing him
my gun. "This will knock his brains through the—" I never
got a chance to say "wall."

Dopey made a lunge for me or my pistol—I don't know
which—but he never reached either one. His ass wasn't four

169

inches up off the sofa when Jhonny's .38 roared three quick times, hammering him to the floor. He lay crumpled near Karl's feet underneath the window, mouth open, tongue hanging out, eyes caught in permanent surprise. His body twitched for what seemed minutes but was really only a second or two. Then the dogs were on him in a frenzy, strangling on their snarls, teeth tearing at his limp, rag-doll body in animal fury. I expected him to cry out in pain. He couldn't—he was dead.

My heart was trying to burst out of my chest and my stomach was squeezing out of my ass. Karl kicked at the dogs. "Git the fuck away from there!"

They leaped to one side, slinking back to the far corner by the closet, crouching down. Karl stood staring at Dopey's body, the smell of gunpowder in the air, watching the dark red ooze from the dead man's head and creep toward his feet.

"Eh man," he said to his brother, "you almost got me." He laughed a low, crazy laugh.

The four of us lifted the lifeless creature and carried him back through the kitchen into the bathroom, dumping his dead ass in the bathtub, head covering the drain, feet dangling over the opposite rim, and drew the shower curtains closed. I wanted to run I was so scared. My head was racing —what if somebody heard the shots and called the police? What if the narcos had been watching our operation and picked today, Sunday, for a raid? We could get rid of the drugs, but not the corpse. Man, if the police came in now, we'd all be going to jail and never coming out!

I managed to hold myself in check. We spent the next hour cleaning the mess up—so much blood on so many things. We scrubbed the walls, the floor, the furniture, the refrigerator, and ourselves, using water from the kitchen sink, letting dead Dopey have the bathroom all to himself. I went upstairs to change.

Pepper had gone when I entered the apartment. It was stone quiet except for the sound of my feet scuffling down

170

the carpeted hallway. I reached the bedroom and changed in a hurry, eager to get the evidence of murder off my body.

How did it happen? I wondered. It didn't seem real. But the bloodstained clothes piled on the floor said it was. I started back down the hallway wanting to blame Jhonny, Karl, Joe, Dopey, Andre, anybody but me. Shit! I dug that I was thinking like a punk. The motherfucker's dead and it's his own fault! All we got to do is get rid of the body. My heart calmed down and my stomach stretched back into place. Wasn't no sense in being scared! I slammed the door behind me. FUCK HIM!

When I arrived back at the office, I picked up the phone and called Pablo, telling him that I needed his truck for tonight. Karl went to the closet and broke out the blow. "I think the occasion calls for this," he laughed.

Me and Jhonny laughed too, but I didn't see nothing funny. We sat around sniffing coke. drinking Henessey.

And then business went on as usual, people calling and coming over, dropping off cash and picking up their drug supplies. All the while, dead Dopey in the bathtub behind the closed bathroom door.

All the cocaine and brandy were gone by the time Pablo showed with the truck. But wasn't nobody high!

Karl and Joe went with Pablo to dump the stiff after we'd stripped it naked and thrown all identification away. Me and Jhonny went up to my pad to smoke some reefer. We were feeling the coke now and needed something to hold it down. About halfway through my first joint the phone rang. It was Andre.

"Eh, my man." His voice sounded happy.

"Yeah. What's happen'n'?" Mine was dry and flat. He must be calling about his cash, I thought.

"I seen Dopey's wife down in Mandy's this afternoon and she told me she had your cash, so I picked it up for you . . . 16 gran'. She was scared to bring it herself; thought you might kill her. She say Dopey didn't know anything about it, she had it stashed at her mother's. I'd a called you earlier to tell you the good news but I went to see a broad over in New Jersey."

I was getting sick inside.

"I was gonna drop off your gran' tonight but the bitch wore me out. See you in the morning!"

Click!

13 Business was great that summer. No one had come around asking questions about Dopey—he had simply disappeared.

My cash was growing and I made regular trips to upstate to see my wife and kids and stash my cash there, giving Ava and the kids enough to live like queens. I moved them from the dump they were living in to a seven-room apartment, bought new furniture, carpets, and a color TV in every room —including the bathroom. I started a small cab business there and turned it over to Ava to manage. She'd worked for Whitey off and on, and now she could work for herself.

Just because my wife and I were no longer living together, she and my children would not be left like my father had left my mother and me, to scrounge for ourselves, alone and for-gotten. It may not have been my Dad's fault that he had to leave, but I do blame him for not caring after he had gone.

I wanted to surround my family with a wall of cash to protect them from the savage, preying white man. I wanted them to be proud and independent.

✿   ✿   ✿

The phone rang one afternoon when I was alone in the office. I hadn't heard the voice before. It asked for Ruben.

"He ain't here right now. Can I take a message?" I was strictly business.

"Yeah. Tell him that Cisco called and I got something for him. I'd like for him to come up to my house and get it. An' tell him to bring some more with him, double the amount." I got suspicious. How the fuck did I know who I was talking to. Could be the police.

"Can he call you back?"

"Yeah, he's got the number." Then the strange voice calling itself Cisco hung up.

There was something about that call I didn't like; just a feeling, a hunch, nothing I could explain. Ruben came in about twenty minutes later and I told him about the call. He gave me a wide, satisfied grin.

"Oh! That's my man Cisco. He lives uptown in the projects where I used to live—" I interrupted him.

"You never told me about no Cisco. What's he want?" I looked at Ruben hard, questioning him with my eyes. What the fuck was he doing? Going into business for himself?

"I know I didn't tell you. He's a new guy. I gave him a small package two days ago when I was up visiting my wife. He's all right, though. We did time together."

I still had that funny feeling inside.

"How much he owe?"

"Not much . . . three hundred." Ruben was trying to sound confident. He knew he could lose his job for shit like that, giving our merchandise without my okay. He was trying to make it sound good. "He says he can kill 'em uptown with our shit, take over the whole area!"

"All right. Call him back. Tell him to bring the cash."

Ruben made the call, rapped a few minutes, then said he'd be right up. I exploded!

"What the fuck you tell him you coming up there for? You know he sposed to bring the cash to us!" I was really

174

getting pissed off. It was against my policy to send anyone into a strange area to collect or deliver; too much chance for a setup. Unless I had been doing business with the dude for a long time, I had him bring the cash and pick up his merchandise at a place I knew. Ruben was really getting shook up, eyes popping wide, Adam's apple jumping up and down.

"Hey boss, take it easy. I know this guy. He says he's babysitting and can't leave 'cause there's no one to stay with the kids. He's got things sewed up pretty good and he needs the stuff."

I still didn't like it. But maybe I was getting jumpy—things had been going too smooth lately, no busts, not many losses, Andre had been paid, and now we were working on my profit. Maybe my nerves were on edge. Ruben was staring at me, pleading with his sad, brown eyes, begging me to trust his judgment. I gave in.

"Okay, man, but I'm going with you and we ain't taking nothing. We pick up the scratch and that's all. He can get the shit later." I hesitated. I still had some protest inside me. "Why the fuck don't he hire a babysitter?" Ruben's face twisted into a smile. "Aw, c'mon, boss. I want you to meet him anyway, so when he comes and I ain't here you'll know who he is." That made sense. My last resistance fell.

It took us fifteen minutes on the Bronx River Parkway to reach Gun Hill Road, where I made a right after the exit. We caught a red light under the El at White Plains Road, then sped across to Laconia where I made a quick left on squealing tires heading uptown. I was in a hurry. There was no one in the office and I was anxious to get back before I missed too many calls. We were in the better *Negro* section now, flashing past neat one- and two-family houses, mostly brick, some attached with carefully manicured patches of green—subway suburbia within the city limits. These homes belonged mostly to blacks employed by the City of New York—policemen, firemen, sanitationmen, transit workers—

175

with a sprinkling of professionals, like teachers, lawyers, accountants, people whose jobs qualified them for twenty- to thirty-year marriages to the bank.

At 225th Street, the Edenwald Projects loomed on my right like giant silos, quarters for the no-money blacks, Spics, and poor-ass whites who'd got caught in the wrong harvest. I nosed the car in that direction.

I slid the car into a tight parking space and we hopped out, the two of us sharp as sin in Big Apple caps, tight wool knit sweaters, flare-bottom knit pants, and alligator shoes. We found number 1271 and entered. The lobby was filthy, the floor hadn't been mopped in weeks, and the walls were scarred with dirty words. Most of the ceiling lights were out, leaving dark spaces that matched the gaping holes where the mailbox doors should have been. Noisy children were running back and forth, ramming into the work-weary adults, some holding crisp paper bags crammed with food. The adults were too scared or tired to open their mouths and suffered the rough treatment in silence, staring down at the screaming bullies or up at the lighted numbers indicating the elevator's descent to the ground floor.

The indicator flashed a green L and the elevator doors screeched open discharging a fat Puerto Rican woman with rollers in her hair. She barely cleared the door before the crowd made its rush. Ruben and me waited like gentlemen until they packed themselves in, then we pushed in. It smelled pissy, and Ruben mashed number 10. When we stopped at the sixth floor I noticed two men in the right rear corner who looked like they hadn't shaved in weeks. They were dressed like bums and giving us the eye. I nudged Ruben.

"Hey, man," I whispered. "See them two guys in the corner? I think they're bulls."

Ruben checked them with a glance, then whispered out of the side of his mouth: "Could be. We'll get off at ten and walk down to nine to make sure!"

I felt better when one bum got off at the eighth floor.

The elevator door screeched as it wound open like a sardine can, and Ruben and me pushed out onto the tenth floor. We hesitated a second, looking down a long fire-red hallway lined with apartment doors on either side, waiting for the elevator to wind shut. About midway down the hall a thick, glass-block, floor-to-ceiling window gave off a soft light that divided the narrow tunnel into two shades of red. A few feet farther down, on the opposite wall, a red-lit sign said EXIT. We headed for it and bounced down the stairs to the ninth floor.

As I stepped out of the stairwell, a polished silver badge sprang up into my face, followed by a menacing voice.

"HOLD IT!"

I felt a sharp pain in my side as the business end of a snub nosed .38 pushed against my ribs.

"Don't make a move or you're dead!"

I froze, scared to breathe. One of the bums that I'd seen on the elevator stepped around to face me.

"Put your hands on your head, dummy!"

His voice came through a slit in his dirty beard and his blue eyes got cold. I did as I was told. A voice behind me said "you, too," so I knew the same thing was happening to Ruben. Dirty Beard shifted his peacemaker to the small of my back, moved around me, clamped his hand on the back of my neck, and pushed me forward. He forced me over to the adjoining stairwell and ordered me to strip to my drawers. When I hesitated, he cocked his gun to speed me up. If looks could kill, he'd a been a dead motherfucker. I stepped out of my clothes, then he ordered me to stand in the corner.

"FACE THE WALL!" He searched my clothes, then snarled: "DROP YOUR DRAWERS!"

I knew that he was now fucking me over, but I had no choice. I lowered my shorts and stood bare-assed facing the wall.

"All right, turn around and get dressed!"

I did as I was told again, hating this white pig sonofabitch with every breath.

177

Dirty Beard herded me back into the hallway where two more filthy-faces stood with drawn pistols covering Ruben, who was facing the wall, hands clasped above his head.

"This one's clean!" Dirty Beard remarked to his companions. "Bring that one over here. Let's see what it's got!" The other two kept their guns drawn and pointed at me while Ruben went through the same ordeal in the stairwell. I was thinking that the police must be pretty hard up to put guys like these on the payroll. In a few minutes, Dirty Beard pushed out from the stairwell shoving Ruben ahead of him.

"Git over there, next to your partner, and keep your mouths shut," he said pointing toward me with his gun.

The three rabid dogs held a short conference a few feet away, eyeing us all the while. I looked at Ruben, he looked at me. We couldn't hear what they were saying.

"Hey!" Dirty Beard motioned to Ruben with his .38. "Git over here!"

I didn't have to wonder long. They both reappeared in a few seconds but this time Ruben had handcuffs on his wrists.

"Okay, I got it! CUFF THAT ONE TOO!"

After we'd been booked at the Forty-fifth Precinct for possession of dangerous drugs and slammed into a cage, I said quietly to Ruben:

"Hey, man, didn't I tell you not to bring no shit with us. Why'n fuck didn't you listen?"

"Boss," he sighed, "I swear to GOD I didn't have no shit on me! That fuckin' cop lied. He had it stashed an put it on me!" Ruben's eyes filled with tears. "Now I got to go back to jail—for nothin'!"

I didn't know whether to believe him or not. It didn't make any difference, because neither the DA nor the judge would.

"Don't worry man, we'll go see Jimenez and get him to fix it so the case will get thrown out."

At our hearing, bail was set and we were remanded to Bronx County Jail.

While I had been waiting to be processed I had gotten

into an argument with the oncoming duty captain, a black. He'd been telling me that the best thing black people could do in America was vote. I told him the best thing they could do in America was leave it, GIT OUT; that just because blacks helped elect a dude, white or black, he'd better do what the white folks wanted or he'd be out on his ass. I ran a train of examples while he glared red-hot at me, his white compadres looking on and listening. I kept rapping, getting better all the time—black people were a captive people like the Jews in ancient Egypt; he was a slave himself, set up over other brothers locked in cages like animals; white people used Negroes like himself to keep the more aggressive blacks down, and if he couldn't see it he needed to lock himself in a cage.

"Well, smart-ass, I'll see if I can't give you some sense when I get you upstairs." He smashed his right fist into his left palm, twisting his face in anger. "Git your stuff. You're going to the fourth floor!"

I knew I was going to pay with my ass for what I'd said, but I couldn't help telling that overfed, black, ignorant pig what was on my mind. Before he could get me upstairs, where I might not have come back in one piece, Pepper arrived with my bail. He glared at me, gnashing his teeth like a wounded hyena.

"You got away this time but you'll be back. Smart guys like you always come back!"

The office was ransacked when I got back. The police hadn't been there. Everything was gone—the drugs, my pistol, my clothes, and the strongbox with nine hundred dollars, collections from two days before. I asked around questioning some junkies. Karl and Jhonny were seen going in and out and were now in business for themselves—with my drugs!

I caught up with Jhonny late the next evening at his house. His woman, Tina, let me in.

"Hey, man," I asked him, "what's going on?"

His eyes grew wide like a maniac's. "I done took over, MOTHERFUCKER!" he shouted, pulling MY magnum from behind his back. "From now on, YOU works for me!" To make sure I understood, he gave a loud whistle and the two vicious Dobermans came running down the hall and stood stiffly on either side of him, low growls rumbling in their throats.

"You'll get the shit and bring it to me, or else." He was grinning his ass off now in front of his woman, who many times in the past had let me know when he wasn't around that her tail was mine for the asking. I'd always turned her down for fear of Pepper finding out. Now she stood looking first at him then at me, soaking up her revenge, glowing in my humiliation.

"All right man, whatever you say." I ate shit but I didn't intend to digest it. As soon as I got downstairs I puked it up and began plotting the deaths of Jhonny and his brother. I had cash, and contracts could be bought for as little as five hundred.

My plan didn't have time to develop. A few nights later I received a phone call from the cop, Dirty Beard. He offered to shift all the weight onto Ruben and I could go free. He wanted five grand. Who the fuck did he think he was bull-shitting? Even if I was stupid enough to do it, he would just have my five grand and that jive-ass cop would push to get me as much time as he could, plus he would spread the word that I was going to sell out my man so that Ruben would turn against me and give him more information. I decided to play his game—my way!

"Why the fuck didn't you do that in the first place, instead of giving us that shit? If you wanted cash you could have said so. You didn't have to bust us!"

He laughed at that. "If I didn't lay something on you or your buddy, how was I going to get you to pay? Look, I ain't gonna talk on the phone no more. If you want to do business, meet me at the Interlude. Know where it is?"

"Yeah." (What hustler didn't know that spot? The police used it for a drop.)

"Okay, then see you there in a half hour."

180

"Wait a minute—"

"What is it?"

"Was we set up?"

"Talk to you when you get here."

Click! That was enough for me. We HAD been set up! I made up my mind: no more action for a while. The cop could go fuck himself. I was leaving—not leaving town, just changing locations.

The next day, me and Pepper moved in with her mother, who lived in the South Bronx in a block referred to by the *Daily News* as the "worst block in New York City." Nine out of ten persons living there were in some kind of illegal racket—numbers, drugs, shylocking, and some others that I didn't know about. You name it, it was there.

The yards in the backs of the old, worn tenements were so filled with garbage they rivaled the Pelham Bay Dump. Garbage wasn't all that could be found back there. The meat wagon seemed to come almost every week to haul some butchered body away. I was trying to catch a breeze at the window one hot summer night about 3 A.M. when four shots rang out below me. Two dudes came out of the basement next door and entered the building across the street. A few minutes later a bleeding man crawled up from the same basement, pitched over in the gutter and lay there, groaning loudly and begging for help. A loud voice boomed from one of the windows in the building:

"Hey motherfucker, why the hell don't you shut up? You gonna die anyway. People's trying to git some sleep, so hush up the fuckin' noise!"

The meat wagon came for him three hours later. He was stiff as stone.

Life inside the cramped four-room apartment was a jungle, too. Legions of roaches marched across the walls and floors, foraging for food, feasting on what they wanted, and shitting up the rest. Some of them even braved the cold of the refrigerator, often drowning in an open milk container or freezing to death on a fresh stick of butter. The brazen

181

roaches made their homes wherever they pleased, usually nestling their dark brown bodies where it was most comfortable, in the upholstered sofa, the chairs, and our beds.

They were Little Leaguers compared to the ravenous rats, huge rust-colored creatures almost a foot long, with long buck teeth. No food was safe from them unless it was locked in the refrigerator or the metal cabinets high on the walls. Anything left in the storage cabinets under the sink was doomed. A garbage container in the house was an invitation to dinner, so people simply threw their refuse out the window, delivering it airmail to the giant "Rodent Restaurant" in the backyard. I knew I couldn't stay in that apartment long, especially when the rats started using my clothes closet as a day-care center.

I finally made a contact with Jimenez, a slant-eyed, hawk-faced Latin lawyer with a reputation as a fix-it man. His office was across the street from the Criminal Court House in the Bronx. He listened to my story and said he would take care of everything for $3,500 cash.

"Don't worry, Jimmy," he said, licking his thumb and preparing to run his fat, stubby fingers through the pile of crisp, new $100 bills I'd just plunked down on his desk. "You have come to the right man. When you gotta appear again?" He spoke automatically, never stopping the count or diverting his eyes from the cash.

"Next week. Tuesday."

"Okay, I'll be there." He stood up, sliding from behind his desk, and walked me to the door.

"Don't worry."

What the fuck made him think I was worried? He had my thirty-five hundred, didn't he? "This case'll never get to the grand jury!" He smiled, offering me his hand. I took it and pumped twice. It felt like a rotten pork chop.

"Docket numbers 178412 and 178413. James Watson and Ruben Gomez. Violation of State Narcotics law, criminal possession of dangerous drugs." The bailiff was calling our case, it was 10:30 and the fucking Jimenez wasn't there yet. I marched up the aisle followed by Ruben and stood before the judge, a silver-haired, pink-faced dude in a black robe sitting high up on a pedestal behind a dark, walnut altar. He looked down at us like we were a couple of turds and ran some shit about charges. The pompous old fart asked did we have a lawyer or did we need a public defender? I told him I had retained Mr. Jimenez. Where was he? I didn't know. Come back in two weeks with your lawyer. Bail continued.

I burst into Jimenez's office demanding to know why the hell he hadn't shown up. Our case was more complicated than expected, he said, and he asked for $7,000 more. I told him to go to hell, he'd already taken $3,500 and hadn't even budged off his ass to come to court, right across the street!

He flared up, telling me I didn't know how things worked. If I didn't like the way he was handling my case, I could get another lawyer. I said I would, and asked for my money back. He gave me half, saying the other half had been spread around.

"Where," I asked, "around yo' gut?" I jammed my cash in my pocket and slammed the door.

Two days later I made contact with another dude who said $6,500 apiece would do the job. The price was high but he said his work was guaranteed!

He took $3,250 from me, then looked at Ruben. Ruben said he didn't have any money on him now, but he'd come back with the $3,250.

"Wait a minute!" I went out to the car and came back with $3,000. I said to Ruben, "Look, man, I don't expect you to pay it all. Just raise the other half. Okay?"

"Bet," Ruben said.

When we reappeared in court, the new lawyer was waiting.

"Is everything all right?" he asked with a smile. "I mean the money?"

Yes, I told him, everything was "right on." Ruben dropped his head and said he hadn't been able to raise the cash. The lawyer didn't like that and said so!

"Now I'll have to make some changes. You got yours, right?"

"Yeah," I told him, I got mine. "But what you gonna do about the money I gave you for Ruben?"

Ruben's money was still working, he said, but without the full amount Ruben still might have to do some time.

"How much time?" Ruben asked.

The lawyer explained that because of his record he could get seven years. Ruben looked like he wanted to leave right then.

"But," he added, "because of the three grand, we might be able to work something out. . . . A year or two!"

The lawyer went through the doors marked "District Attorney's Office," and when he came out ten minutes later he looked pleased with himself. He'd made the deal—probation for me, one year for Ruben.

"How's that?"

I didn't like it. "Can't you get it thrown out?"

"Look, Jimmy, both you guys got records. A throwout would look funny. The arresting officer is pushing to get you and Ruben some time. You got probation, and you got a year. Take it or leave it!"

I took it. Ruben took it.

We walked downstairs, and when we got outside the lawyer asked where the money was. In the car.

"Well, I'm going to have lunch in that kosher restaurant across the street. Meet me there."

At 2 o'clock we all went back to the courthouse. The lawyer stopped off at the DA's office and told us to go inside the courtroom and wait. We sat and watched a black judge sentence niggers and Spics to jail left and right. I wondered if my rabbi was selling us out.

He whisked into the courtroom forty-five minutes later and sat next to me.

184

"It's all set. Go up to the third floor, Part Four, and wait. We got a different judge. This guy won't go along with it because it'll look like he's showing you guys favoritism. He's black, you're black, so he's got to be hard!"

Up at Part Four, the bailiff called our names. The lawyer said that at this time his clients would like to change their plea to guilty to lesser charges. The assistant DA spoke up saying that he would accept it because we weren't such bad guys.

"Mr. Watson did not have possession of drugs upon his person when he was arrested!" he added.

That knocked me for a loop. Here they were admitting that I was guilty of nothing and accepting a guilty plea for something I didn't do. I'd made the deal but I knew that I was getting fucked for what they knew they couldn't prove. That's the way the police, the courts, the judges play—pay or go to jail.

The judge made his speech about no one promising us anything for a reduced plea. We said "NO" and pleaded guilty to the lesser charges. The judge set sentencing for the next week, Tuesday, pending a probation report.

The probation officer made me recite my life history, and when he asked me if I was married I told him yes.

"How does your wife enjoy you sexually?" he asked.

"How does your MAMMY enjoy you?" and I walked out. The lawyer told me later the bastard had recommended I go to jail. Dig that shit!

At 1 o'clock Tuesday, Ruben and me entered the Bronx Supreme Court building. At 1:45 I walked out with three years' probation. Ruben got a year in jail.

I had survived.

✻   ✻   ✻

Things had to change now that I was on probation. If I fucked around now and got caught, I wouldn't have enough

185

cash to get out of trouble. A few weeks before I'd gotten busted, I'd bought a home upstate, in the country, new furniture, the works!

Damn! I was glad as hell I hadn't gone to jail. I had to enjoy that house, do some living in it, had to know what it felt like. I'd never even slept in it. I wanted time to think, to get away from everybody in the hustlin' crowd. No one knew me or what I did upstate.

Upstate—FREE! No cops! No stickup man! No .38 under my pillow! No pressure hustlin' to pay Andre or Stan. I ate well and slept sound.

I always felt good whenever I went up to visit my family. I became a family man; sporting Ava and the kids to the movies or out shopping or just riding around, taking in the scenery. Being with them was important. I loved Pepper, but I wasn't gonna do what my mother and father had done: "Went off with another woman after he left us . . . raised her kids an sent 'em to college . . . never did SHIT for you! YOU GONNA BE JUST LIKE HIM!"

For the first time in a long while, Ava seemed almost happy. Not that she acted any more alive in the new house. She still dragged around and complained that she felt tired all the time, but there was a faint intensity in her smile, and to my amazement she was anxious for us to get out and socialize with her new friends in the area.

One friend in particular, Hilda, was always ready to break out the booze, the reefer, and some heavy sex talk. Hilda called almost every day, inviting us out to her place. It wasn't long before Ava's zest for socializing petered out, and out of boredom I began to drop in on Hilda by myself. We'd get high and talk.

One evening Hilda and me discussed my wife. Hilda was telling me how close she felt to her and casually let out that Ava owed her money.

"Ava owes you what?"

"Two hundred and sixty-five dollars!"

"What the fuck she owe you that kinda money for?"

"Man, I don't know. She called me and said she needed the bread, man. So I sent it to her."

"Well, I don't know why she had to ask you for scratch when she gets $150 to $200 a week from me to live on, just to eat and shit. I pay all the bills."

Hilda looked fortyish but claimed thirty-six, a dyed blonde whose body lumped where it should have slumped and slumped where it should have lumped. In clothes—her flesh rolled underneath as she moved—a walrus in motion. Her face was a blush of fat feminity, oval, chubby, and cute. Sharp hazel eyes that lied, schemed, smiled, bewitched and cried on her demand. Smart, racist, and rich.

Hilda loved, craved, demanded black affection, sex, and drugs.

Hilda sniffed horse. I had some left and sold it to her. The good shit off the top. She could afford it and told me so.

She also wanted to dine on me and was doing everything short of offering me her fortune if she could but wrap her lips around my penis and draw out the black nectar in its root. She wanted us "to be friends" she said. She was supposed to be Ava's friend.

Now Hilda was sitting in her kitchen looking up at me from a table littered with business papers, cookies, reefer-paper, reefer, jelly stains, used paper cups, and the beer cans we were sipping from. The ash tray was spilling over with butts, roaches, and ashes, an accumulation of two or three days.

"I love that little girl of yours. She's so sweet."

Now my wife was a little girl.

"Maybe she's using stuff," she went on. "I don't know."

That shot through me—all the unpaid bills, her sleepiness, her loss of weight, her fucked up complexion, her tenseness. That was it!

The realization came rolling in on me like the Red Ball Express, nonstop, bringing everything with it.

"You know that she's been using stuff?"

It was more my pronouncement than a question.

187

"No. I never did it with her, but she told me the night of the closing on the house when we were down to Boo Boo's celebrating that she had been strung out once. She started crying—"

"Yeah, I remember ya'll said she was crying because she was happy."

"Well, she was happy and scared, because she had been fucking up and you had bought her that beautiful house and you was bound to find out now because you'd be home more."

"Find out that she used drugs?"

"I don't know. Every time you'd get up from our table that night she'd cry, saying what a wonderful husband and father you had been to her and the kids."

Hilda's round, pink face was flushed. She went on, all restraint gone now.

"Didn't you know, man? You're in the business."

How the fuck was I supposed to know? I schooled the shit outa her, taught her about the drug business and never to fuck with anything you couldn't cut loose—letting her know that I was risking my ass with that shit because I wanted her and my children financially secure.

Bought them a house upstate, in the Catskill Mountains, moved them out of the dirty city, air and space and green trees, and got them a legitimate business, a respectable business.

The car, the business, a home, and money stored away, buying everything except the house with cash. I'd shot other niggers, paid off cops, kept others making cash for me and themselves. Riding around hooked up with a pistol, watching for the stickup man with one eye, the narco with the other, and needing a third to find the dudes that owed money. All three things at one time—all that—for her to be a junkie!

I slammed my fist on the table, making everything jump and fall.

"Please, Jimmy, take it easy," Hilda pleaded softly, her lips

188

puckered and pushing each word gently to me, blinking her eyes. She didn't fool me. She thought my mounting anger would explode on her ass, so she was doing the oldest number in the female book when faced with an enraged male: Get feminine, sexy, offer him the tail, siphon off his anger through his prick.

"See you later, Hilda. Ava's got some explaining to do."

"Don't tell her you got it from me. We're such close friends, and I wouldn't want to hurt her. God, why did I do it, what made me tell you?"

"Aw, come off it. You know why you told me. Shit, who else could know but you?"

"Jimmy, I really don't know why!"

"Think about it, baby. It'll come to yuh. See you later."

My whole body was numb as I pushed my legs, forcing them to carry me out of Hilda's kitchen into the living room with the big picture window. The window during the day was a live nature study in moving color, looking out over a little stream that twisted and circled through the trees down the hill from the house. But it was night now, and the blackness had erased that charming scene, leaving only a mirror in the window, which as I looked into its blackness reflected a distorted me—shorter, with a bigger head, and arms too long for my body. I felt like the reflection, all fucked up.

*　*　*

The full realization came the next morning—safe deposit box, empty!—bankbooks, closed out!—insurance policies, canceled! Everything was gone. I WAS BROKE!

Ava didn't offer any explanations. She just said she was "sorry," packed up, and took the kids with her down to Alma's house.

I stumbled through the week crushed, in a state of despair. All that hustlin', what had it come to? Broke and on probation, with a house I couldn't pay for, no family, a

189

record. OH, GOD, is this your punishment? OH, LORD! OH, LORD!

By Monday morning I'd pulled myself together. The Lord or nothing else was gonna help me with me shut up in the house, wailing like an old woman. I had to make some moves, find me a job or something. Not just any kind of job, I'd been to college—I'd even worked for CBS and been on television. Maybe I could hook that up again.

I called Mike at his old CBS number and was told he no longer worked there—my hopes began sinking—but he was now working for radio station WRVR at Riverside Church.

I reached Mike that evening before he went on the air. He sounded really surprised to hear from me and agreed to meet with me the next night.

"Okay, Mike, I'll be coming in from Great Neck. Got terrific story for you. Drug dealer's wife shoots up all his money. See you at the church tomorrow night, my man."

The idea had come to me while talking to him. What if I could get him to write my story? I got in my car and headed for Great Neck. I hadn't seen LaVaughn in a long time.

14 As my big Olds cruised toward where Wendy would be waiting for us, I gave LaVaughn more background on Mike.

"Baby, I'm telling you this guy I can't believe. If you'd known him three years ago and saw him now—he's beautiful."

"Oh, yeah? Why?"

"Long story. Used to be a big-time dude at CBS. I used to work for him."

She was only half-listening, searching the dark streets for Wendy. Suddenly she spied her. "Stop. There she is."

"Hey, baby."

"Hi. Pull up some; there's a lot of dog shit around here."

The three-foot-wide green island which ran the entire length of Sham Avenue separating curb from sidewalk was spiked down with oversized trees and saturated with dog shit.

Wendy picked her way across the island and got in. I continued on about Mike as I pulled away.

"Like I was saying, this dude is either on a fad or he's for real. I hope he's real. Anyway, that's why I asked Wendy to come along. He may want to go out, but I really would rather talk. With women around a guy's either going to come on strong with his dick or his mind."

"Right?"

"Right."

"So then I'll know whether he's really down, or just a sex-bent head freak. I've been thinking seriously about doing a book."

"That's what you been saying all week. But, honey, if you write all that stuff about drugs, won't you get in trouble?"

"Here, Wendy, light this joint. I ain't plannin' on writing it myself, baby. That's why I'm going to see this dude Mike again. He's a journalist. I'm gonna find out from him tonight if he's interested in writing my story. I didn't say nothing about it when I seen him last week . . . just told him 'bout Ava, set him to thinking. Gimme a blow."

I pushed down hard on the accelerator and roared onto the expressway, speeding for the city. We made a quick stop to pick up reefer from No-Ko and then drove on up to Mike's pad on Riverside Drive.

"Come in. Come in." Mike answered the buzzer with a triumphant flourish, ogling the girls approvingly as we stepped into his living room. Acid rock blared from a boss stereo set, and daring posters hung on the walls, posters of love and freedom. One I remember best—two lovely women, bare-breasted, one sucking the other's tit.

"Man, I got some out-of-sight grass. Have some of this."

I took the joint Mike had been smoking. He took the girls' coats. I was high already, but I had been smoking pot long enough to know good pot when I tasted it, and this was class-A garbage. I made a crack about how bad it was. Mike got peeved, so I offered him a joint of No-Ko's smoke. Once he took hold of it, that joint worked its magic. He thought he was the only person in the room who was high. I laughed.

192

"The girls are stoned," I whispered. He dug that.

"That's great, man. What's next?" He was glowing with anticipation.

I dropped down on the rug, drawing LaVaughn down with me. Now was as good a time as any to say what was on my mind.

"I got an idea, my man. Why don't we do a book together?"

For a moment Mike's expression became almost serene as he looked at me. Damn, did I sound like a fool to him? Did he pity me?

"I'll get us all a drink." He smiled. "I want to hear more about your idea, Jimmy. I've been thinking about writing a book myself."

I felt LaVaughn's hand close tightly around mine.

* * *

Walking to work. Down the soft elevator from the eleventh floor, through the ornate marble and mahogany lobby, and out into the crisp wind off the Hudson River and the noontime sunshine, which in Manhattan shines brightest on Riverside Drive and its tagalong park, through which I walked the twenty blocks to Riverside Church, listening to the birds; cross at 120th Street, a short turn onto Claremont Avenue, enter at the back of the church, three steps down into a basement mezzanine, soothed and ready for another day in the great radio experiment, WRVR, 106.7 on the FM dial. Oh, it was going to take every liberty granted by the First Amendment, the full-page announcement in the *New York Times* said on the day we started!

WRVR had been for years a nonprofit classical music station run by Riverside Church, a vast thud of a cement block of wealthy Waspishness right across the street from America's most boring national monument, Grant's Tomb. Now the station was commercial, although still owned by the church, and it was supposed to be an all-news, public affairs radio station, full of news of the counter culture, the

193

radicals, revolutionaries, minorities, disfranchised—the no-holds-barred, say-what-you-like, and tell-it-like-it-is radio, staffed by a cross-fertilizing blend of disenchanted newsmen with big-time experience and young beginners with energetic fervor to try new types of radio journalism. We all assumed each other shared the conviction that commercial broadcasting had become a corporate servant posing as the people's informant, lulling its listeners and viewers into the false conviction that they were finding out what was going on in the country.

A walk to work—in Manhattan, for Chrissake!!!—no longer encased in my Richard Bennett photometric-tailored gray suit with the little red and white pinstripe and the large lapels, high center vent, and a trifle of a bell where the pants broke over the Florsheim demiboot; but now in jeans with a green and red butterfly sewn on the right leg by my twelve-year-old daughter, who was making Daddy beautiful, and a pair of scuffed Western boots whose leather heels cracked out the pealing of the freedom bell with every striding step I took on the asphalt of the park path.

Walking to work, humming inside, feeling loose, making money, too, $22,500 a year—not much, of course, in terms of New York commercial broadcasting, and a big drop from the CBS paycheck I had become accustomed to. But comfortable. It helped support the family, which lived in the old apartment, allowed me my own three-room apartment five blocks away on Riverside Drive, and left enough for modest restaurant dinners, occasional ski trips, life insurance, telephone bills, utility bills, sales taxes, and all the rest of the devices that keep us all—you too—on the inflow-outflow treadmill.

The new people running RVR had worked under me at WCBS-TV News. I had hired them as innovators, and they had been fired by CBS shortly after I was deposed as News Director, along with most of the other people I had hired. They had been stained by their association with me. The old story: If there was no union to protect individuals, corpora-

194

tions brought them in and threw them out, like tires on a truck, with only the fleetingest thought to disrupted lives and shattered dreams.

So now, people who had worked for me were my superiors, not I theirs, and that was good. It represented the standing of habitual values on their heads, part of my personal process of liberation. Challenge the values, face them, stand them on their heads, survive the change, and emerge freed from them. Little symbols: Doormen no longer snapped to attention when I strolled up now in longish hair, suede jacket, scuffed boots, slower stride, an ambling posture. Suspicion now, sometimes hostility. The less snapping to attention I received, the less important it became. Yes, just plain folks.

Sometimes incense on my desk at RVR during the frantic hours my producer and I put together the ninety-minute news broadcast I anchored each weekday night, keeping me up there in their fumes, staying attuned to the larger issues as I sifted through reams of United Press International wire copy full of the propaganda, lies, trivia of the day. The stories nearly always missing the point, selecting those that I would rewrite for the broadcast, giving them the personal point of view that was our specialty. We aired no "objective" news on "RVR/Evening." We found a point in every story, and it usually wasn't the same one the wire service writer had found, or was allowed to find.

There was little significant information in those yards of paper that unfolded each day from the UPI teletypes. Garbled accounts of the daily violence in America, lies from Washington, Albany, and City Hall, and stereotypes about anyone else with the misfortune to be caught up in the great American news machine. The daily stories from Vietnam carried none of the thump of bombs, the bursting of bodies and the shrieks of the dying. They were glib accounts, full of monstrous Pentagon euphemisms for death and destruction, daily dissimulations, lies that during a decade of exposure had been identified publicly for what they were but that were still being used by the arrogant weapons-dealers, bagmen, fixers, legislators-for-hire, and coagulating generals who had taken over the soul of government.

All of the meaningless words from United Press International filled up the newspapers and radio and television stations each day everywhere in the land. Yack, yack, yack, yack, and dazed people all over the country wandering about, silently asking each other with tortured eyes: What's going on?

The ninety-minute broadcast felt good to do. The public events of the day we treated as the continuing surreal adventure of a nation whose culture was being throttled by the uncaring greed of its people. Our audience was small, the facilities ancient and inadequate, the technical support amateurish, but on that ninety-minute broadcast I felt my journalistic work connected with my experience in living the reality of life in this country. It was the first time in years I did not feel an aggravating split between the two. It was no longer schizojournalism. I counted my blessings.

My new apartment was working out well, too. It was sometimes lonely living alone for the first time in my life, but it was also a heady freedom, a stimulating time. I dealt only with myself, came and went as I pleased, invited women over to spend the night, and discovered to my delight that the unfamiliar solitude was spurring me creatively and spiritually. I meditated deeper and longer than I ever had, ate and drank less, and in my time off from the radio station began to write better than I ever had.

And now Jimmy Watson was coming by. I had seen him only once since our CBS days. That time he had treated me to a night on hustler town. Then two weeks ago the phone on my desk at RVR rang and there was that unmistakable voice, guarded by the sense of danger in talking over the telephone to whoever might be tapping the line—the FBI, perhaps, or the New York City cops, or the District Attorney of New York County, or maybe the Bronx, or Kings County, or Queens, the U.S. Bureau of Narcotics Control, the Mafia, who knows? During his infrequent calls I wondered how he could exist out there without exploding in his world of constant protective tension, to be surrounded with the knowledge that Attica State Prison was hovering in his reality, that the man he dealt with yesterday might kill him tonight, unless he killed him first.

Jimmy and I had dinner together last week as a result of that call, and I knew he was startled and pleased with the changes he saw in me. I was pleased to see him, too, because for six months I had been tracking him down. I wanted to write a book, my first, and I wanted him as the subject of it. I didn't mention it at dinner last week. I would tonight.

The phone rang.

"Hello, Mike?" It was Jimmy. "Be there soon. I got two girls with me. That all right?"

"Sure. Come on. I had about given you up."

Two girls with him, huh. A twinge in the lower part of my abdomen, surprising me with the adolescent speed of the reaction. Horny. Well, we would be socializing tonight, as well as tending to business. I wondered what that would be like. And who would the women be?

The buzzer rasped—had to get that awful noise changed—and there they were, three of them, teeth and personalities sparkling with the glitter edge of the cocaine they had been sniffing; Jimmy dressed like a swagger stick, upthrusting leading edges of the thigh muscles arching the upper legs of the leather pants, coming in the door, throwing his leather cap on the top of the left speaker of the stereo that the aged Jewish neighbors already were complaining about, pumping out Whitey rock singed to a loving red by the acid creativity of the middle-class musicians. And in he came with his calculated walk, front of the feet outthrust to the outside edge, hunching a bit, looking around deftly—had to be quick to catch his swift appraisal, that worried wrinkle when he noticed the uncurtained windows open to whatever eyes might choose to pry from the building across the street. Narcs, perhaps, with a long lens and a camera. Looking fly and partying, he was. The two women, young and beautiful, hair care-

197

fully in ringlets, tailored pants cut high and snug over the slightly swinging hips, lashes and makeup and scent—had to be an hour and a half's worth of preparation on each one.

Only their youth, their color, and the pepper of the hip flick muddied the image of two CBS wives arriving at a house in Larchmont pledging their fealty to Mr. and Mrs. Newly Arrived Boss holding their first reception for the subordinates. They seemed bourgeois and anxious, too focused on self to extend warmth to others. Their attractiveness made that doubly disappointing.

But they were festive, their grooming was festive, and it was not long before their spirit took me along with them.

So down on the rug—no furniture in the apartment—and out with the grass, which I touted, and after a few draws Jimmy pronounced the smoke trivial, his judgment delivered with the weight of a Brazilian coffee buyer dismissing the village's crop as unworthy of purchase. He was gracelessly showing off in front of the women, asserting superiority in dope matters. Unnecessary and irritating. I responded in kind, criticizing his ego necessity of always having to have dope that was better than anyone else's.

After that flutter of machismo combat, the evening settled in and Jimmy and I began our first long and searching talk about ourselves and our relationship. As the talk went on, fueled by occasional sniffs of Jimmy's cocaine, excitement mounted in both of us. Parallels in our experiences kept jumping out; mutual interest in each other's stories; areas of conflict were slipped by with ease. And then, incredibly, Jimmy said he wanted me to do a book with him.

Throughout the talk, LaVaughn and Wendy sat a few feet away from us, silent, talking neither to each other nor to us, smiling vaguely when I would send a little joke their way, being discomfited by my role of gracious host—pouring a glass of Malaga for Wendy, chablis for LaVaughn, and fruit juice for Jimmy, who ignored them except for the few times when he would turn to LaVaughn and say: "That right, baby?"

198

And she would nod affirmatively in silence.

Pouring wine in the kitchen, I asked Jimmy about the girls in the other room.

"Are they hookers, Jimmy, or what?"

The hurt that swam up into the backs of Jimmy's eyes rested there only a moment.

"No, man." He forced a little grunt of a laugh. "LaVaughn's my woman out on Long Island. Wendy's her friend. They're just here, man."

From time to time I would turn toward them, try to draw them into a conversation. They would answer vaguely and briefly with a nervous smile, and Jimmy would come in quickly, resuming our conversation. Once I leaned back my head onto Wendy's thigh and felt only the tenseness of her muscle, which didn't move.

No connections.

I sensed them looking at me as though I were a man from another planet. And when we looked at each other it was across a treeless plane of race, class, age, history, mutually puzzled, and Jimmy, equally uneasy, took pains to keep it that way.

About 4 in the morning, our heads began to short-circuit with the accumulations of cocaine, grass, wine, and exhaustion. Conversation slowed to a trickle, and eyelids drooped, and it was time for making love or sleep. Sleep obviously was the choice.

Before ending the evening, I suggested to Jimmy that he be the subject of a radio documentary I wanted to do on the life of a drug hustler. It would be a good way of starting the book project as well. He agreed to come by the station the following week to begin taping.

When the women stood to leave, Wendy was weaving. Jimmy had been feeding them coke throughout the night, and Wendy had never passed up a sniff. Now, too late, she realized she had had too much. I told her she could stay if she wished, but she mumbled painfully that she needed some air. I opened the door for them, said good night, and crashed into bed.

Late the next morning, as I returned from the grocery store with breakfast in a paper bag, the building superintendent stopped me at the elevator.

"There was a godawful mess in the hall on your floor this morning," he said in his Swedish accent.

"A mess?"

"Yes. Someone threw up all over the hall, right in front of Mrs. Levy's door. She stepped into it when she went out this morning. The others on the floor think it's the new tenant. The doorman said some people came down from your apartment very late. Know anything about it?"

"No, I don't and I'm sorry to hear about it. I certainly hope it wasn't anyone who was in my apartment last night. If someone got sick they should have cleaned it up."

"Yes. We're very clean people around here, you know."

"I'm glad to hear it," and I abruptly pushed the button summoning the elevator, wanting no further hassles in this apartment building that I had taken such pains to find.

The elevator door opened. I punched my floor and rode up, furious now. Why the fuck did they let that dame throw up all over the fucking hall? Why the fuck didn't Jimmy knock on my door and we could have cleaned up the goddamn mess instead of letting that little old lady who spent four-fifths of her day dusting her apartment step into the stinking shit?

Goddammit! Fucking niggers!

❖   ❖   ❖

It was 9:05 P.M. The broadcast had been over five minutes, and I was back at my desk filing away the rundown of the evening's show, looking over tomorrow's calendar. The buzzer on the door leading into the station from the main hallway of Riverside Church caught the copyboy as he hurried down the hall. Pulling open the door, he glanced briefly

200

and unseeingly at the black face atop the stocky body and passed on. Jimmy slipped inside the door and waited in the hall, seeking out the corner that had the least light. I glanced over—I had been expecting him—motioned him to wait while I finished my paperwork. I did not invite him to step from the hall into the newsroom. There were people there, and they would be curious. The fewer people he met, the fewer the questions, and the easier it would be to carry out our work that night—a clandestine taping while Jimmy went about his business. Jimmy liked the hallway corner he chose. He did not like to be lit and looked at by white folks.

I finished with my papers, grabbed my jacket off the hook, my small SONY tape recorder off the desk, out the door, through the church lobby, to the street, and into Jimmy's car, a long and ornate Eldorado, tan, a hustler car with seats that slid with the touch of a button, forward and backward, tilted in and out, and soul from the stereo speakers in the back.

"Let's go."

15 Across Manhattan through Harlem, Jimmy pointing out to me on the East Side the youngsters, eight, nine, ten years old, lounging in doorways waiting to sell marijuana to the automobile trade—reefer curb service —then over the Triboro Bridge into the grim streets of the South Bronx, driving carefully, easy, Jimmy's eyes always flicking, left, right, rear-view mirror, picking up everything, the traffic in front and behind, the people on the sidewalks on both sides of the street, the passing police cruisers becoming more numerous every time we came into an area where drugs- and numbers-hustling was high. Like crows circling a dead groundhog by the highway, the police sniffed the money.

"Look at this place, man." And I looked, seeing only empty, littered, stinking streets, grimy and sagging buildings, many of them gaping in abandonment, lit by the sooty yellow of the street lights, the only periodic color crimson and purple neon signs saying "Bar."

"Numbers and dope. That's all that goes on."

Jimmy was in and out of the bars, quickly, then stopping at the curb occasionally, summoning someone over for a few grunts of business talk, doing his rounds, handling neither cash nor dope, staying clean. He had on his person only the expensive hustler reefer—$60 to $100 an ounce sold only by Puerto Ricans—reefer that turned the senses and the intellect onto full-perception mode, followed by cocaine to get our tongues wagging.

We smoked and sniffed, and I took out my tape recorder. With a question here and an interjection there, I got Jimmy talking about the dope business as we drove through the city:

"When times are good everybody is making money. Like the bartender, the numbers writer, even the landlord is happy because he knows he's goin' to get his rent money. He ain't going to get no story. There's less violence, less people getting killed, beat up. People are in a gayer mood.

"The greatest problem in their life, you know, is surviving, surviving financially. And when they're surviving, people just seem to overflow, out of the tenements, onto the streets, into the bars. People rub shoulders and talk: 'Say, my man, how you doin'? Ain't seen you in a long time. How are things going?' You can buy him a drink.

"You understand what I'm saying, Mike? Like you feel the whole thing is alive. But when The Man come and start tightening down, cracking down on the drugs, well what happens is there's less money in circulation. It's like you're stopping that life vein, the thing that lets the people express their joy. People's problems loom even larger because half the things they got they got on credit. When there's no money, there's nothing, nothing happening. There's no emotion.

"When things are going people on welfare can have color TVs, can eat good steaks, that stuff. Because the drug addicts go out and bring these fruits into the area, fruits that aren't there because people can't buy them. People ain't going to buy color TVs because they ain't got the money. But the people get 'em because junkies go downtown and steal 'em and bring 'em back. So then *you* got 'em.

"Maaan," Jimmy was feeling expansive now, stretching the

203

vowel, gripping the steering wheel of the car, piloting it nimbly, "just to go somewheres, just the feeling of being able to move. That only comes when there's money in the area.

"Now it seems like when people want to start containing people, putting people back in line, they take their money out of the area. Because, let's face it, everybody know how the economy is run in the black community. The economy there ain't run by people going downtown and bringing their cash back and spending it in the black community. First of all they ain't getting that much, and what they earn they spend back downtown.

"But when you got the numbers going for you, or drugs, or something like that, you got some chance of getting some money. And The Man knows what you're doing in the neighborhood. He knows that you're writing numbers, that you are doing something to make a living. Right? And that's his living too. He lives off it.

"So really, the vice, the drugs that goes on in the black community allows the business in the black community to survive. It's a whole system of everybody having their place and living. And once The Man takes that away from you then you have more violence, more everything. Everybody got to start that scratching and pecking thing. And the strong going to take off the weak."

We had left the South Bronx now, heading north into another part of the borough. Less garbage on the streets, trees occasionally, more open, less furtive; a light rain had started. We were on our way to meet Marvin, a friend of Jimmy's, a man on the periphery of show business who made his basic living dealing occasionally in drugs—cocaine or heroine. Jimmy was going to put together such a deal tonight, a small one, to help his friend.

We pulled up at Marvin's apartment building, a large unrelieved square. Only the doorman distinguished it from public housing. The architectural drabness was the same.

204

"Yes, sir? Whom do you want?" the doorman queried us in the lobby, and tension surfaced in Jimmy, filling the small enclosure like the acrid smell of gunpowder among the plastic plants.

He might have been a prison guard, and Jimmy the prisoner heading for the box.

Jimmy mumbled Marvin's name, barely keeping himself under control. The doorman buzzed upstairs, we were let in —Jimmy smoldering and softly cursing "fucking doormen." The doorman had not been unpleasant. He had even been gracious. Doing his job. Jimmy saw him as a pompous and humiliating peeping tom and an obstruction. He never seemed to get used to doormen and they knocked him off his otherwise confident stride. Uniforms, keys, and petty authority—especially with a black face—angered Jimmy, raising his hackles, bringing forth a blue-steel glint. Dangerous.

He knew this danger in him, and it was one of the reasons he avoided white people, and why if stopped by a cop for even a traffic infraction the situation was heavy with peril for each. Jimmy's violence was bubbling silently just under the third layer of skin, waiting to gush forth. I sensed and understood this in him because in that we were the same.

But since my boisterous teen-age days I rarely encountered situations that provoked that spirit within me. I was white, transmitted an aura of power, and probably the lurking violence. People didn't mess with me. Jimmy was a black man driving around in fine clothes and a long car, conspicuous, drawing to him the racist anger in policemen and other servants of white authority. They yearned, lusted, got a hard on at the prospect of grinding him, humiliating him. If the wrong cop stopped Jimmy at the wrong time and said the wrong thing, someone might die. That tension always traveled with him on the streets, and I feared for him.

"Why don't you get a Volkswagen?" I said to him one day, only half-jokingly.

Marvin opened the door of the apartment in response to

205

our ring, and his eyes grew wide when he saw my white
face behind Jimmy's. Jimmy spoke quickly, easing his friend's
sudden fear.

"This is my man Mike. The guy I told you about. He's
all right."

Marvin had served time twice. Once more and it would
be forever. That knowledge sapped his strength. You could
taste the caution, the wariness, the fear in him.

Marvin smiled at me and shook my hand limply as I entered the room, furnished heavily and bright with primary
colors and African artifacts. Another friend, calmer, was sitting on the long sofa. We said hello, and I sat in a chair in
the corner, leaving the sofa to the other three.

Out came Jimmy's cocaine again, welcomed with brightened faces. Everybody sniffed, and the three of them began
to rap. They made no effort to draw me into the conversation. I sat back and watched, making no effort to get in. I
didn't belong there, and everyone knew it. But I was Jimmy's
man and accepted as that. The discomfort was palpable in
the room, but there was nothing to be done about it.

Not only discomfort, but a pervasive nervousness. I kept
expecting a heavy knock on the door. Continuing motions
with the hands, constantly roving eyes, quick looks my way
that always avoided my gaze. Especially Marvin. He was up
and down, over and around, laughing, talking, always moving, dancing on his toes, ready to flee.

The conversation swirled through jokes, women, business,
tonight's deal, sports, and money. Money figured in every
statement, remark, exchange.

"Mike thinks I talk too much about money," Jimmy told
his friends with a wide grin. "I tell him, man, money is
where it's at, Jim. Moneyyyyyyy. You gotta git some for
yourself."

Which brought on a hilarious rap, all of them tumbling over
each other's words with their money stories and money
jokes. It went on for fifteen minutes, the three of them
looking at me with amusement. Yes, Whitey can disparage

money because he gets it easy. But we don't knock it. It's our goddamn, fucking lifeblood! We got no money we go to jail!

The agreement concluded, we left in separate cars to make the night's deal. A cocaine deal—Jimmy and me in his car, Marvin and the other man in Marvin's car.

As we pulled away from the curb, I reached beneath the front seat, pulled out the tape recorder, and invited Jimmy to resume the conversation:

"A kid, you know, would rather hustle drugs than snatch a pocketbook. You can more make money that way. Plus it's not a crime, man, among certain people to hustle drugs. Because *where're* the drug addicts going to get it? They need it. They want it. They got to have a source. So the whole thing creates its own business.

"When you cut off the drugs then people got to find some way of keeping their living up, so they resorts to the butch off. And then you have guys start to sell fake drugs. And then the addicts are looking for him. You got a lot of problems, because money becomes like blood. People fight and die over money, man.

"The drugs cool out the community, man. If they didn't why the hell did they fight them wars to send opium into China? You cool the populace. I mean right after you had the riots in Watts drugs became plentiful. It cools people.

"Drugs is money, man. You can have more than one form of money. You can print it up or it can come in those little glassine envelopes. Somebody want it.

"If a guy can't sell drugs, he's going to do something else. He can't get no job. What kind of job he's going to get? Half the people got records. Who's going to hire them?"

Jimmy snorted with disdain. And both of us had another touch of coke, dipping into the folded dollar bill with the cover of a matchbook folded into the form of a scoop, sniffing up a scoopful in each nostril. We had reached the rendezvous point, and Jimmy pulled over to the curb and shut off the engine and lights.

"If you take the guy that used to be a junkie and you cool him out on methadone and you still don't give him a job, he's still got to get money. Right? What you're doing is sticking a pistol in his hand. He learned all that in jail anyway.

"If you didn't have drugs to blame problems on, then maybe you would look. You'd get back to the things you're trying to avoid—housing, jobs, life-styles, living conditions in general."

He stopped talking suddenly and looked at me sharply. We were talking in the front seat of his car, James Brown thrumming on the stereo tape deck. I was holding my tape recorder in my lap and leaning over with my right arm extended, holding the microphone toward his mouth. It was visible from the street.

"Hey man, I'm just thinking. You know if somebody sees me here talking to this white guy holding a microphone, both of us are gonna get killed!"

The danger of what we were doing had been in my mind, but far back. Yes, we were not being discreet. Should we be spotted by either police or hustler, Jimmy would be assumed to be blowing the whistle on the dope dealers or the cops and the politicians who lived off them. The Knapp Commission was riding high in New York then, and much of their work was based on information given by informants. It was dangerous for us. Fifty dollars could buy you a hit man in New York.

I put the tape recorder down on the floor of the car for a while to let both of us cool off from our sudden realization.

We talked of this and that for a few moments, then Marvin's car pulled behind ours. The headlights flicked.

Jimmy got out, strolled over to Marvin's car, got in the back seat, talked for a few minutes, and money changed hands. He got out, came back to his own car. Deal completed, a successful venture. Profit: $300 for each man.

We drove off, and a few blocks later I took out the tape recorder again, this time holding the microphone below window level.

"Where was the drug pusher in Vietnam? How did all them guys get hooked? I mean where was the evil guy over there making them soldiers who was fighting for their country, for everything they believed in, what made them start using drugs, man? Was it some evil, vicious, criminal pusher? Or was it the conditions that they have? I think we brought that kind of ill with us. We sent guys 10,000 miles from home and they got hooked. So what is this, you know? What is it? This is what I'm trying to find out. This is the question we're asking. Can you believe that drugs is really the problem?

"Why do people keep smoking cigarettes? You tell 'em it's going to give them cancer. Why do they keep doing it?

"They like it!

"I don't guess you can tell people what to like and what not to like, you know. I don't think so."

We stopped for a light, and across the street, down the sidewalk, came three dudes, about sixteen or seventeen, black with full-brimmed hats and multicolored bands encircling them. Sharp. Tight jackets over fitted black pants. One of them had his arm wound round the shoulders of a cuddling girl; everyone was strutting, looking fly, having a good time, hoping they were being observed, on the town. Jimmy looked over at them.

"Now look at these kids there. They're wearing hats like the hustler hats and everything. That's what them guys want. You ain't going to tell those guys about no Boy Scouts. A young guy like that with his woman wrapped up with him, he's a man! He feel like a man. If he had a shot at it, he's getting some drugs, getting him a car, getting him some pool playing. He'd take it."

The light changed, and we moved on again. Getting on toward dawn now, the post-nasal drip from the cocaine making our voices hoarse, our minds tiring.

"Let's face it. The same people who control everything, you think they wouldn't control a multibillion dollar thing like drugs? You think they're going to let that kind of

209

money get away from them? Come on, man, it don't make sense. So all the while we run around chasin' our tails. The dog is chasin' its tail."

Jimmy roared with laughter at the image of the American population running around chasing its tail while the bankers and the politicians stashed away their money.

"Oh, man. Who we locking up? All the blacks and Puerto Ricans who is using drugs and selling drugs. We ain't busting down on the people who are putting up that big money to get it in here. I mean, you know, look at the money that has to go up to get this thing. Ain't no black guy got that kind of money. Right? Who are the ones that go to jail? Constantly. Every day. Who they picking up? Who are staying behind bars, then come out and don't say anything?

"Like I say, you know, there's a market for it, man! People want it! People demand it! Just like selling pussy. Somebody always going to buy some pussy. A guy with a wife at home, he goin' to buy some pussy.

"And everybody, like, hates the police. The police are hustlers themselves. But they can hide. They ain't really taking chances. Now, though, they got to take chances to get their money 'cause they don't know if the next cop is a Knapp Commission guy. So they getting real straight now, coming down on everybody. Like, all the while before, when everybody was a brother, hah, there was even a camaraderie about them just rippin' off your cash. It was a big joke! They taking it out there to the suburbs and living good. They really down with whatever crime was happening. They're the real criminals. And they's really punks too. Because we can go to jail. They have their badge, they don't go to jail. So now if there's any threat to them they hide behind their badge. They act straight then, you know. They start bustin' down on you harder.

"So, like, there ain't nobody that digs the police, because they drives around looking for trouble to make a profit. Just like the people been saying: You can get mugged, robbed, raped, anything—right?—and a policeman is never around. They's always around a numbers spot. They's always around anywhere they can get a dollar. You're getting beaten, mugged, raped, or something, that ain't going to get them no dollar so they're not interested in that. They ain't the defenders of the law or nuthin'. They're moneybrokers, crimebrokers. They're dealers in the very thing they are supposed to be against. And they're punks about it because they been doing it with a license—with a gun and a badge, and that's a license, you know."

Jimmy was puffed with anger now, anger at the white authority which hovered always over his life, keeping him from doing what they did themselves.

"Even if a guy really can't deal heroin no more, he's going to do something, you know. And I don't think he'll be going back to the Establishment."

❋   ❋   ❋

It was near dawn when I dropped Mike off, drove back to Great Neck, and pulled into my underground garage. I shut off the motor and sat there, smoking and thinking.

Well, I'd taken the first step. From now on there would be no turning back—I was finished as a hustler. How long was it gonna take Marvin to spread the word to Stan and Andre that I was hanging 'round with some white reporter. Marvin knew who Keating was. From now on them guys wouldn't trust me as far as they could spit. That was all right. I didn't owe them and they didn't owe me. I just hoped they wouldn't get the idea I was informing on them. Maybe I should tell them to listen to the broadcast. Was Mike really gonna put that tape on the air? If he did, a whole lotta people wasn't gonna like what I said, especially the police. And there would be others who would say that fucking pusher's just making a case for his self, trying to justify what he's been doing.

So, shit, maybe I was. Who don't? What the fuck was I supposed to do, just come on out over the radio and tell

211

folks how guilty I'd always felt whenever I looked at my children and knew they knew I was dealing heroin, the drug that television commercials said was killing kids their ages, or how a piggish sensation of greed always pricked at my skin whenever I stood, sharp as a motherfucker, in some swollen-arm junkie's apartment watching him count out the cash to me while his junkie wife and baby sat looking on with hunger in their bellies, or that my mother had lost her pride in me, or that my own wife had become a junkie? Who the fuck cared or could do anything about it? I mighta been justifying, but I wasn't crying.

I didn't feel no shame; I'd gone for a bullshit dream. Stan wasn't big time, neither was Andre; wasn't no black hustler big time. We was all hustlin' for The Man, taking our places on his millwheel and gradually having the life ground from our bodies—to feed The Man, keep his courts, jails, and safe deposit boxes filled—to support his Long Island homes and Westchester estates.

Yeah, I had believed in the freedom of the almighty dollar, and in the end the police, judges, lawyers had snatched that freedom from me because it was only an illusion.

Well, maybe I'd always be grabbing at illusions. But when I find something that ain't, I'm gonna hold on real tight!

*　*　*

My energy was fast dropping toward zero when Jimmy left me at my apartment. I headed immediately for bed and four or five hours of sleep before I was due at the station to prepare that evening's show.

Despite the fatigue, I was chafing to begin editing the hours of conversation we had recorded. I would build a ninety-minute broadcast around them. The tapes were powerful, aching with truth. What Jimmy had said from his perspective made electric connections with the perspective I had drawn from my experiences.

Such as the night, standing in the middle of the campus

at Columbia University, the dark pierced by the campus streetlights and the floodlights brought by the police. The sense of disintegration and confusion I felt.

I had been wakened in the night by a phone call from a young friend who worked at the university.

"You've got to come up here and see this," she said on the phone, a hysterical edge sharpening her soft tone, a sob underneath. "Come now. It's horrible."

I knew without her telling me that the expected police bust had occurred at Columbia. All week students had been in control of the campus, occupying buildings, vandalizing the offices of officials, letting loose their anger over the war that was taking their peers as cannon fodder, angry with the university's profitable and comfortable affiliations with the weapons-makers, angry over their sense of helplessness in controlling their own destiny. The university had been effectively shut down, and all over New York elders were puffing with rage at the youthful anarchy. As each day went by there was in the air an escalating demand for a crackdown, for revenge.

Now the police had come.

I lived only ten blocks away, had often strolled through the campus on sunny days listening to the speeches and the singers. I was there within twenty minutes, my press card gaining me admittance through the barriers police had erected around the campus, and I skirted the hooves of the mounted police who were charging the crowd gathered on Broadway outside the gates, a crowd full of fury at what had gone on inside.

I arrived too late for the main police surge into the occupied buildings. I was in time for the mopping-up operation.

The campus was now under control of the police. But cops continued to prowl the territory, forcing stragglers into clusters, which then were assaulted by club-wielding policemen, the numbers on their shields covered with black tape to prevent identification and a charge of brutality. Students in the groups who could not flee because of the crush or

213

who attempted to defend themselves were hauled off by the hair of their heads and hurled into the police wagons with a final club stroke across their backs.

I had seen many police actions as a reporter and through that experience had learned not to be squeamish about the violence often necessary in an arrest; I was aware of the dangers faced by policemen. I also had developed an eye for effective police control of crowds and often admired the skill and cool of New York policemen, handling angry war protests in the city. I had been an officer in the navy, had been at sea, and was familiar with the look, smell, and sound of maddened men out of organization control. The police on the Columbia campus that night were out of control. They were not bringing order to the campus. They were venting their own hostilities and hatreds, escalating the violence, teaching lessons. A microcosm of peace with honor in Vietnam. Adults brutalizing the young, shouting up at stunned students peering from dormitory windows:

"Go back to yer mammy, punk!"

"Why dontcha call yer daddy!"

A ragtag band of a half-dozen girls from Barnard, very young, was led out of a building, being escorted off the campus. As they came out of the building onto the broad walkway they began to pipe in quavering voices, exhausted young faces sallow under the floodlights, "We Shall Overcome." I was touched and amused by their little gesture. And as they approached the main gates a dozen burly patrolmen being mustered into a bus to head back to their precinct hooted at the girls, and then, in their blue uniforms with black masks over the tops of their silver badges, helmets on their heads, handcuffs and guns dangling from their belts, truncheons in their hands, they began to bellow "America the Beautiful."

Disintegration and confusion. Standing there watching, listening to the two songs bouncing off each other, baritone and soprano, each side singing louder to the other, I knew that this was a moment that would remain with me, form my future thoughts, one of those events you sense as personally historic immediately upon its happening. Similar to San Francisco, when I was covering the Republican National Convention for the *New York Herald Tribune* and a cop put a hostile, restraining hand on me on the convention floor. It was the first time a cop had interfered with me, the press, and I was noisily outraged. That convention nominated Barry Goldwater. Reporters today have been going to jail. It's old stuff now.

Yes, the police had become a political movement, under the bumper-sticker campaign slogan "SUPPORT YOUR LOCAL POLICE."

Sure . . . support your local police. Christ, nothing would make me more comfortable than being able to rely on the police, to feel protected by them on the streets at night, to know that my children were safe in going around the city.

But the police are ideologues now, not peace officers, and the noisy ideology serves to obscure the other reality, their failure as traditional policemen and their emergence as a criminal syndicate.

And sitting day after day in the Association of the Bar of the City of New York building, broadcasting live over WRVR the public hearings of the Knapp Commission to Investigate Police Corruption, I listened to the dismal testimony of cops, turncoats, undercover agents, criminals, all describing a police department with a gigantic hand out for money—cops selling heroin, cops planting evidence on the innocent and arresting them to make a quota or to rid themselves of individuals who might inform on their rackets, sleek cops with big homes in all-white suburbs shaking down struggling Puerto Ricans who keep their stores open on Sunday in the ghettos, cops spending their duty time seeking out gamblers and inviting them to operate in their precincts to increase the size of the graft pools from which all the precinct personnel drew their monthly allowance, cops stealing, cheating, abusing, in a manner so open and flagrant that the entire force—the nation's largest and known as "New York's finest"

215

—was involved, either themselves stealing or approving those who did. And City Hall knowing but not acting, frightened by the political power of the police, a power given them by the white people of New York who regarded the cops as the last line of defense against their own children and the menacing niggers. Blinded by their hate, the people could not see or did not care that the upholders of law and order were looting the city, not protecting it.

Disorder and confusion.

And remembering now those days when I was a youthful legislative correspondent in Albany, capital of the State of New York, sitting around the bars, the hotel suites, sharing too many drinks with legislative leaders and chairmen of legislative committees, listening with sophisticated amusement to the stories of the bagmen dispensing money to the Solons for votes on special-interest legislation, which is the main activity of state legislatures. Never actually seeing money change hands, mind you, but watching legislators reverse themselves after visits from lobbyists, mostly representing business and industry, and I would smile back at the knowing winks sent my way after the vote switches. And knowing in detail the way state legislators arranged laws to benefit their businesses; and observing day after day the bills and the debates conducted under the fluttering flag of the American way and the preservation of the free enterprise system but which had as their purpose the elimination of competition and the setting up of profitable, legally protected steals for those who had paid their money to those who had the people's votes.

The state legislature was a place where the sharks arranged to tear more flesh off the taxpaying fish—the weaker the fish, the larger the chunks bitten off. And the court system, our great American system of equal justice for all. Shit, that was the primary obscenity in the legislature. Most of the legislators were lawyers, and with the exception of a few their interest was the law businesses. They dragged their asses to Albany each year for three months to cop a lot of money for

216

themselves, or a judgeship, preferably both. If you dug deeply enough into the political machinations surrounding the vote on an important piece of legislation, you invariably found a legislative leader or a county chairman hustling a judgeship for his cousin, his bagman, or the man who gave him money.

For someone to reach the bench in New York State, where everyone must stand in respect when the judge enters to take his seat in front of the American flag, a man must wade through a sludge of kickbacks, payoffs, hypocrisy, theft, doublecross. In Albany, the senators and assemblymen lined up in their nice suits and glittering fingernails, drooling on the crimson rugs, staining the leather chairs and sofas, waiting their turn.

Was I shocked, appalled, nauseated, scandalized by the experience? Well, listen: I was not one of those delicate academicians flowering in the ivy and lilies of a university; I was not an ivory-skinned priest taking dainty nourishment from his breviary illuminated by the afternoon sunlight slanting through the stained-glass windows. No, no, I was a knockabout big-city reporter, boozing and carousing with the Solons, living with the warts and farts of the political system, and liking many of the politicians, who were hypocritical only with those who elected them, not with each other or the press.

I wrote my share of exposés—even got cursed out one day on the floor of the State Senate by the Majority Leader—but those stories seemed essentially an internal exercise, to make my editors happy with their choice of reporter, to make my fellow reporters respectful and envious, and to make legislators fear me and therefore try to please me by giving me information I wanted. I never expected the readers to march on Albany and drive the thieves out of the temple, and, of course, they never did. If they had I would have thought them fools.

All of us—reporter, editor, reader—operated on the assumption that there were rotten apples in otherwise healthy barrels. Catch the rotten apples in legislatures, courts, police departments, business, government, throw them out, and all is well again. No one except cranks and Communists proposed the idea that an entire legislature could be malevolent; that a President—a President, for Chrissake!—could be motivated solely and exclusively by his desire to be re-elected; that the primary objective of a municipal government might be enrichment of the officeholders, not public service; that politicians, attorneys general, presidents, governors, lawyers, judges, corporate executives, policemen, generals, admirals, sergeants, reverends, quarterbacks—that all of them, the very top leaves of American society, might well have and often do have as their motivating life force the amassing of money, not the fucking commonweal!

So I didn't always see what I observed. That's the reality of big-time democratic government, I told myself, and others told me so as well. And basic to this acceptance of things as they were was my conviction that, in the end, in the long run, the system worked. So the legislators lined their pockets and the bums got promoted, and the courts were filled with greedy hypocrites, and businessmen would rip the rings off your mother, but weren't we all living better? Weren't we all freer, healthier? Were we not, despite it all, perfecting ourselves?

And what in fact would you substitute for our system? What? Stalin?

Yes, of course. Despite all the flaws and contradictions, the general direction of the country was benevolent, producing a society better than any other. That's what I used to believe. Everyone I knew believed the same. And if you didn't believe it, buddy, you'd be out on your ass without a job! There were certain assumptions demanded of wage-earners, and America the Beautiful was the main one.

And personally the system seemed to be working for me —marriage, family, work, all a success.

I could not now point to a moment in time when accumulated realizations forced me to meet myself. Probably there

218

was no such moment: It was more like a pecking-away at an elaborate structure, changing its form, never causing it to tumble entirely, but diminishing its size.

Oh, there are certain things. The discovery of the starving poor in the '60s and the meanness of the public response to the discovery; the movement into the higher echelons of journalism and the discovery that the closer one approached the core the more apparent it became that money was the stuff that controlled the essential decisions; racism; the hypocrisy of the Christian religion; those wily drugs, and—lest we forget—the Vietnam War, which I lived through from beginning to end, an event that I first accepted as one of those temporary aberrations, a mistake by the CIA soon to be corrected. But as it grew in dimension along with my children I began to question harder the country, its people, and myself—Oh, God, it was agony!—and discovered a people absolutely, fanatically entranced with its own bullshit; a people allegedly independent, talking big but enslaved by that paycheck. Support your government, boy, or it's no job and the welfare line for you! So everyone decided not to notice that the country was in the dank flowering time of the American psyche, a beer belly nation masturbating in front of its television set, hating its children, honoring its thieves and hypocrites, sending its mercenaries and hapless dropouts to rape, pillage, burn, maim, and kill the weak, while gnawing on a T-bone steak.

As I said, there was no specific moment in time when something extraordinary happened to me. Just accumulation. And I sensed myself drowning along with the society in which I was immersed. My culture was dying, and I had to save myself now, to try and find a life that felt organically right to me, even though it flew in the face of all that training in obedience to moral precepts, respect for the law, faith in the intrinsic goodness of democratic institutions, social and personal responsibility, belief in the existence of relative social value of individuals according to education and social class. All of that training, I realized, was the same as that

219

received by the manipulators of our society. They understood me, and I now understood them. They knew how to confuse people like me, how to get into my white mind and tingle my biases and play upon my hopes. Clever fellows who knew how to take all those values that I had been imbued with and turn them grotesquely on their ends and in a maddening doublespeak penetrate my head with rational explanations and justifications to make me buy a product I didn't need and could not afford or to make me accept acts that in my gut I knew were horrible and against life. They could kill for peace and make me believe in them!

Yes, what Jimmy had said into my tape recorder on our long night's ride communicated directly to me now. It felt true, and I was content with the evening's work.

* * *

Jimmy and I had many long conversations afterward, and I came to believe that in many ways his philosophy was more appropriate to our times than mine. For a lifetime he had looked up at the white man from the perspective of the sidewalk, watching those long legs walk by in their tweeds, blue uniforms, workers' coveralls, often looking for nappy heads to grind under their cordovans. Jimmy's wisdom came from that experience; not much of it came from books, lectures, conversations with the intelligentsia. His knowledge of America, which means white America, was intuitive and raw from the kicks and the curses. He did not need a rational analysis to see reality.

Talking about the heroin trade with Jimmy:

"Look, man. You got this multibillion-dollar trade across all kinds of international boundaries. You think these governments are not involved? Come on, man. How else you think it could work? It's not the Mafia, man. The government is the Mafia!"

Of course. Of course. It had to be. This heavy-volume traffic across international borders in a marketing system so

220

efficient that it is easier to find a bag of heroin on a night-time New York street than it is to find a quart of milk.

You didn't need an international investigation and fourteen volumes of data to know that Jimmy's analysis was on the mark. And now articles and books have begun to appear detailing the involvement of the American, French, and Asian governments in the heroin trade, detailing the influence of heroin profits in the conduct of the war in Indochina. Probably in a while—maybe not in our lifetime—a historian will postulate the thesis that the purpose of the war was not to prop up teetering dominoes and save us all from Godless communism but to control the heroin trade. Trade, after all, has been at the root of most wars in history.

Another night, Jimmy and I, sitting across from each other at his kitchen table, talking about Nixon's decision to mine the harbor at Haiphong and the Russians threatening retaliatory action:

"Hah. The Russians and the Americans going around snarling like they going to rumble. They all down with copping some cash, man. Who they think they bullshitting?"

16 My participation in the WRVR radio experiment lasted eight months. It was the first time I had worked in the medium, and I enjoyed learning it.

But the promises of a place wide open to the development of new forms of radio journalism and new forms of creative interrelationships among the staff and the management turned out to be mostly advertising copy. Few of the people there were really interested in that. They just wanted a format that could compete with the other commercial stations in the city.

It was a boring game I no longer wanted to play. So I left. This time, however, I decided not to exit quietly as I had at CBS. I did it theatrically, made an adventure of it. On my last night on the air I told my audience the whole story and invited them to call in with their reactions, which they did.

KEATING QUITS WRVR IN 'IDEOLOGICAL' HASSLE WITH MANAGEMENT ON NEWS

(Headline, *Variety*, April 19, 1972.)

This time change was pleasure, not trauma.

*　*　*

A year has passed since we began writing this book together, and now we're concluding it. It's not the conclusion we had planned originally.

Halfway through the writing of this book we had decided how it would end: It would end with the story of the new Jimmy, established in a different town, different business, legitimate, accepted, looking optimistically toward the future, and all that, tasting some of the gentleness that life had rarely offered him. Certainly that was what he was looking for, and it seemed for a time that he would achieve it.

"Instead of the wolf, I'll play the fox," he said.

But at that halfway point, life for Jimmy decided to take another turn, and, since this book is about that life, and mine, it turned too. Violence, which follows Jimmy as a shadow, stuck its thumb in his eye again, and he was forced to leave upstate and New York and disappear. He may or may not be back.

It was an early morning telephone call, and I awoke to its ring groggy after a pleasure night of smoking and loving. The woman beside me arose quicker than I and answered it.

"It's Jimmy," she said as she handed me the phone.

"Good morning, Jimmy," I said, trying to brighten my thick tongue.

"You heard?"

I assumed he was questioning me about the reactions of the editor to some manuscript of his I had delivered.

"He thought the stuff was good. Everything looks fine."

"No, I don't mean that. I mean have you heard about what's happened?"

"No, man! What's happened?"

"I'm calling from far away. I had to leave. They're both looking for me, man; the police and some other people. If

223

the police get me and put me in a cell, the people won't let me get out alive—" A plaintive note emerged in his voice. "It's all over, man; all my dreams—"

He didn't talk long, and the details of the sudden turn of events have to be omitted here for his safety.

I hung up the phone, stared a few moments at the mobile hanging from the ceiling representing the universe in ying and yang, and silently left the bed for the bathroom, easing into the realization of the disaster with the mundane routine of the morning—showering, shaving, and preparing to cope with an unknown day. My woman stayed in bed, knowing a dark time had descended that was not her affair. She heard me through the closed door of the bathroom:

"Fuck!"

Our book was only half done, and the next few weeks was a reeling of my mind trying to figure out whether I should tell the remainder of the story by myself or drop the project, or what. And I felt Jimmy's pain—he had talked often about his feeling of never having completed anything. It was a self-inflicted wound, because surely he had completed many things. He was after all fully alive. But he seemed often to feel adrift in currents that petered out, and failure to complete the book would be to him an ultimate confirmation of his self-analysis. Oh, it must have been hurting!

But the wolf-fox managed after a month to regain his balance, to find yet another life for himself, and he re-established communication with me. He had succeeded in getting away. Now he would wait out the problem, watch and feel its development, and determine the degree of his safety.

In time the situation began to look not as perilous as it had first seemed. While that calming process was under way, we resumed work on the book, not as we had done before in those long conversations and drives around town, walks in the woods, and parties and closeness, but through another process, distant and cumbersome and expensive, a process that has brought us to this point.

Part of the process was U.S. Mail. "It seems ironic that

my future and possibly my life is resting in your lap, White Man," he wrote.

In the introduction, I mentioned that Jimmy and I decided when we started this book that we would not first design a structure then fit the book to it. We decided to let it grow like a tree, responding to its own gestalt. This we have done, and being honest to that concept, this is to inform you that the tree is still growing and that this ending is being imposed not because the plant has reached fruition but only because we feel the time has come to end this book.

I told Jimmy a month ago when he was hemming and hawing about needing more time to write this scene and that episode:

"C'mon Jimmy, we have to finish the fucking book. Our relationship keeps changing and developing. This book could go on for the rest of our lives. We've just got to end it. I'm getting tired of it. I want to do something else now."

Something else now. Not that I have any great plans. Hardly any at all. I don't think I've had so few plans since childhood. And so few grand views of the world and where I fit in, or where anyone else fits in for that matter. Judgments don't come so glibly these days, and I make as few as possible, especially moral ones. I trust them the least. Experience and intuition and feelings, when you can find them —those serve better, more trustworthy.

We're happy with growing the tree and hope it keeps flourishing. It's not the kind of tree that I had envisioned. It is not one of those soaring dramas I see sometimes in the Green Mountains of Vermont where I love to ski and breathe. This tree seems more like one of those heroes in the slim mall that separates the northbound traffic from the southbound on upper Broadway outside my apartment building, trees that lick off their parched lips the stray rays of sunshine that pierce the yellowed air hanging between the big stone buildings that line the street, trees that instruct their few gray leaves not to inhale too deeply of the excrement from the buses, cars, motorcycles, bicycles, drunks gasping on the benches, and the crusted mounds of dog turds on the scrabbling ground beneath their bony limbs. A city tree, in other words, right out there in the middle of the street, soaking up the pizza and dry cleaner fumes, sucking its thin tough juices from the leftover breaths in the subway beneath its roots. A tree for '73.

✿ ✿ ✿

JIMMY'S FINALE (a letter)

My Man,

It is morning now; hot and muggy. A robin is hopping cheerily along the fender of an old faded car in the shade of a leaning pecan tree. His brethren blue jays, mocking birds, and spotted tails form the early bird chorus; chirping happily, fluttering from one high branch to the next. The trees are dense. The greenness is thick and buttered with sunshine. This is the last day.

My front yard is a maze of flowers; morning glories, snow on the mountains, touch-me-nots, prissy feathers, old maids. Still moist with dew they sprout in clusters, spilling reds, whites, blues, pinks, purples, yellows above the glistening grass. I should go to the well and draw some water for the old lady up the road. But this is the last day.

Old Triblett sees me now, stretches his long black body, falls back down quickly to scratch a flea, then lies there looking at me, anticipating last night's leftovers. He sort'a adopted me after Joe got killed. I sure miss my dog. Only Pepper remains; everything else from the old hustlin' life is gone. Makes me think, my man: When will she be gone?

The currents of life shift, continuously changing; voids are made and are filled; there is birth and there is death. Tomorrow cannot be born until today is a memory. Two long fishing poles lie close together, drying on the woodpile. I think of you, me, and the river. I think too that this is the last day.

226

I don't think about our friendship, Mike; I don't think about the sun, I'm just glad it's up there. I feel better not trying to probe into what we've shared together, searching for some universal meaning; a truth we could present to ourselves or to the world. If there is anything in what we've done, it will be found. We have sowed and only need the rain to grow. It will come. The clouds will form tomorrow for today is the last day. And what about tomorrow? I'm going fishing today.

May the Gods bless you too,

Jimmy

Message from the President

"Let others spend their time dealing with the murky, small, unimportant, vicious little things. We have spent our time and will spend our time building a better world."

(President Nixon on Watergate, August 1, 1973.)